1985

To Ralph Henry

Love from
Mom and Dad

KANSAS PRAIRIE WILDFLOWERS

Kansas Prairie Wildflowers

CLENTON E. OWENSBY

IOWA STATE UNIVERSITY PRESS / AMES

To **Kling L. Anderson,** who
gave so much of himself to me
and to countless others

Clenton E. Owensby received the B.S.
degree from New Mexico State University
and the Ph.D. degree from Kansas State
University, both in Range Management. He
is currently Professor of Range Management in the Department of Agronomy, Kansas State University.

Composed and printed by The Iowa State University Press, Ames, Iowa 50010

First edition, 1980

**Library of Congress Cataloging in Publi-
cation Data**

Owensby, Clenton E 1940–
  Kansas prairie wildflowers.

  Bibliography: p.
  Includes index.
  1. Wild   flowers—Kansas—Identification.   2.
Prairie flora—Kansas—Identification. 1. Title.
QK161.095   582.13´09781   80–1779

ISBN 0–8138–0850–2

CONTENTS

INTRODUCTION

AMONG the many aesthetic qualities of Kansas grasslands, prairie wildflowers stand out as perhaps the most striking. Even the casual observer is taken by the diversity and beauty of those wildflowers, put there by nature and blooming in successive waves throughout the growing season. A more discerning look at the prairies of Kansas reveals even more, as each new day brings forth different, sometimes delicately minute, wildflowers. Studying them is addictive, and once hooked on prairie wildflowers, the novice seeks materials that will aid in their identification. Unfortunately, the layperson has few sources to use. Those available are usually highly technical and are intended for use by trained botanists. The purpose of this book is to provide an identification tool for those with a limited background in botany. The keys are centered around flower color and gross morphological characters, allowing the reader to narrow the choices, with a comparison of color photographs to make the final choice.

Included for each species in this book are a color photograph, distribution map, plant description, flowering date, and medicinal or edible properties.

Species of vascular plants in Kansas number some 1800 to 2000. I have chosen a relative few representing the showy, common prairie wildflowers. Many species found in and around Kansas prairies are not native prairie plants and so are not included in this book. The major universities in Kansas can and will aid in the identification of such species.

I wish to express my most sincere gratitude to Dr. Annehara Tatschl for her advice, help in editing, and constructive criticism in preparation of this book.

I also would like to acknowledge the assistance of Dr. John Launchbaugh and Mr. Carroll Lange for photographs they obtained for me and to Dr. Spencer Tomb for editing the final version.

Appreciation is expressed to Carol Baldwin Blocksome and Melody Moore for reference collection and typing, respectively.

I also would like to acknowledge financial aid given by the Wichita Historical Museum Association.

Lastly, I appreciate the encouragement of my wife, Juanita, and my children, who make life worthwhile.

KANSAS PRAIRIE WILDFLOWERS

Generalized Native Vegetation Types of Kansas

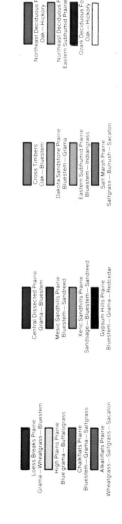

Loess Breaks Prairie
Grama — Wheatgrass — Bluestem

High Plains Prairie
Blue grama — Buffalograss

Chalkflats Prairie
Bluestem — Grama — Saltgrass

Alkaliflats Prairie
Wheatgrass — Saltgrass — Sacaton

Central Dissected Prairie
Grama — Bluestem

Mesic Sandhills Prairie
Bluestem — Sandreed

Xeric Sandhills Prairie
Sandsage — Bluestem — Sandreed

Gypsum Hills Prairie
Bluestem — Grama — Redcedar

Cross Timbers
Oak — Bluestem

Dakota Sandstone Prairie
Bluestem — Grama

Eastern Subhumid Prairie
Bluestem — Indiangrass

Salt Marsh Prairie
Saltgrass — Bulrush — Sacaton

Northeast Deciduous Forest
Oak — Hickory

Northeast Deciduous Forest
Eastern Subhumid Prairie Mosaic

Ozark Deciduous Forest
Oak — Hickory

KANSAS PRAIRIES

Kansas prairies vary from shortgrass in the west to tallgrass in the east with mixtures of short-, mid-, and tallgrasses interspersed between. The diversity of prairie types, each with its own particular flora, gives rise to large numbers of prairie wildflowers. Pristine prairie types for Kansas are indicated on the map opposite.

Mosaic of Eastern Subhumid Prairie and Northeast Deciduous Forest

This area lies east of the Flint Hills in what was originally tallgrass prairie. While much has been plowed, remnants remain. Because of lack of fire, those remnants are dominated by Kentucky bluegrass and woody species. Naturally, the area was dominated by big bluestem, indiangrass, and switchgrass along with other less abundant grasses and numerous perennial wildflowers. Many species of wildflowers once prominent there are rarely seen, since little burning occurs and the plow has long since reduced their habitat.

Eastern Subhumid Prairie

The Kansas Flint Hills remain as the only extensive area of tallgrass prairie in the eastern Great Plains. Largely because of rocky soils, most of the region has escaped the plow and exists now as the home of domestic livestock. Fire was an important ecological force in shaping the composition of the varied plant communities that exist there, favoring warm-season perennial grasses and their attendant wildflower populations. Big bluestem and indiangrass dominate those plant communities, with other tall- and midgrasses being subordinate. Wildflowers grow in profusion throughout the region, sometimes appearing as a veritable flower garden. The landscape varies from rugged, rocky hillsides to flat or rolling uplands to lowland stream areas. That diversity in topography and the resultant plant communities afford many suitable niches for different plant species.

Central Dissected Prairie

As one goes west in Kansas, tallgrasses slowly give way to mid- and shortgrasses which are more drought tolerant. Central Kansas is dominated by mixtures of bluestems and gramas. The gently rolling to flat topography of the region has blue grama and little bluestem as the primary dominants. More mesic sites, such as the Dakota Sandstone Prairie, may contain a fairly high percentage of tallgrasses. Those areas still left in prairie support domestic livestock, primarily a cow-calf type. Heavy grazing on the area causes buffalograss to dominate and usually reduces forb populations. Soils of the region with lime to the surface usually have little bluestem as a dominant, but clayey soils have buffalograss, blue grama, and western wheatgrass. Areas with limestone outcropping generally support many more wildflowers than the clayey regions.

High Plains Prairie

Occurring in the high plains of Kansas where precipitation is minimal, the bluegrama-buffalograss type is a true shortgrass area. The terrain is dominated by expansive flat plains with occasional drainage cuts. The area has a cow-calf type livestock operation, and much of the land has been plowed for wheat and irrigation farming. Areas in the region that have been overgrazed are almost pure buffalograss stands with few wildflowers.

Xeric and Mesic Sandhills Prairie

Along the larger rivers of western and central Kansas large areas with sandy soils exist. An anomaly in the dry west, they produce tallgrass communities and are rich in prairie wildflowers. Sand bluestem, sand lovegrass, and little bluestem dominate the well-attended pastures of the Mesic Sandhills Prairie. Sand sagebrush dominates much of the Xeric Sandhills

3

Prairie due to fire suppression and no control efforts. Sandy areas are excellent for prairie wildflowers in the late spring and summer.

Gypsum Hills Prairie

The Gypsum Hills area in south-central Kansas has a unique topography and a luxuriant flora. The soils vary from clay to sand and are bright red in color. The topography is rugged and the scenic beauty splendid. The dominant grasses vary from buffalo–blue grama to big bluestem–little bluestem. Wildflower hunting in this region is a treat.

PRAIRIE WILDFLOWER ECOLOGY

Seasonality

Within a plant community there is competition for the essentials of life, i.e., water, nutrients, light. During the hot middle summer months no plant competes better for those essentials than the warm-season perennial grasses. The wildflowers are few during that period. The bulk of the prairie wildflowers complete their flowering prior to or after the rapid growth period of the perennial grasses. Even so, there is a wide diversity of flowering dates for the wildflowers, and at no time during the growing season is something not blooming.

Ecological Niches

Finding a particular plant the first time is likely luck, but by noting the environmental circumstances where it occurs, you should be able to find many more of that species. Plants inhabit ecological niches—that combination of physical conditions and interacting flora and fauna providing the necessary elements for successful completion of a plant's life cycle. Certain plants must have shade or a sandy soil. Others may require some specific element in the soil, as does creamy poi

sonvetch which must have selenium in the soil or it will not grow there. Typically, rocky areas are more conducive to prairie wildflowers than are upland clayey soils. Knowing where to look for a given plant is half the battle; take careful note of the area in which a plant grows.

PLANT NOMENCLATURE

Two general name types are given to most plants, the common and the scientific. While many plants may have the same or similar common name, each individual species has but one scientific name. Those scientific names are standardized by professional plant taxonomists using rules published in the *International Code of Botanical Nomenclature.* On a regional basis lists have been developed for a specified area. Scientific nomenclature and plant distributions in this book follow the *Atlas of the Flora of the Great Plains.*

Scientific Name

The scientific name is made up of three or more parts: (1) the genus or generic name, (2) the species or specific epithet, (3) the subspecies or varietal name, and (4) the authority. The genus is always capitalized and italicized, while the specific epithet and varietal or subspecies names are not capitalized, but are italicized. Authority designations indicate the person or persons naming a given plant and are not italicized. An example would be: *Vicia americana* var. *minor* Hook.

Common Names

The common name of a given plant is seldom universal but may differ from place to place or within a given locality. Frequently several different species have the same common name because of some similar characteristic. In Kansas, Anderson and Owensby (1969) have attempted to standardize common names of a selected list of plants;

4

that list will be used as a basis for common names in this book.

Common names, in most instances, are binomial, with a given generic common name combined with a species common name. For instance, the genus, *Baptisia,* has a common name of wildindigo; the species, *B. leucophaea,* has "plains" as its common name, while the common name of *B. australis* var. *minor* is "blue." The standardized common names for those two species would be "plains wildindigo" and "blue wildindigo," respectively. Often a single common name, not binomial in nature, may be so ingrained into the literature that it is used. Two groups of species within a given genus may also have different standardized generic names, i.e., *Astragalus* species that are poisonous are called loco or poisonvetch, and those not poisonous are called milkvetch.

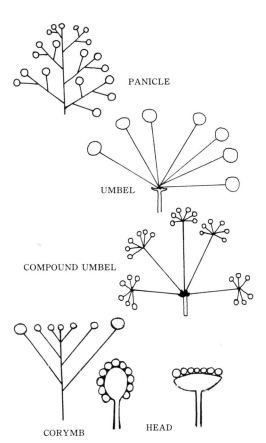

PANICLE

UMBEL

COMPOUND UMBEL

CORYMB   HEAD

PLANT MORPHOLOGY

Identification of prairie wildflowers necessitates a fundamental knowledge of the various plant parts. Often, plants with a similar inflorescence and flower type can be differentiated from each other by leaf or stem characteristics, and vice versa. Careful study of the following line drawings of flower, leaf, stem, and root characteristics will minimize the time required in identifying a prairie wildflower.

Flowers

INFLORESCENCE TYPES

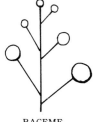

SPIKE   RACEME

Spike—an elongated flower cluster with each flower attached directly (no stalk) to a central stalk.

Raceme—an elongated cluster of flowers arranged singly along a central stalk, each flower with its own small stalk.

Panicle—an elongated, branched flower cluster.

Umbel—a flower cluster in which all individual flower stalks originate from the same point.

Compound umbel—a flower cluster in which umbellate flower clusters arise from stalks arranged in an umbellate manner.

Corymb—a flat or convex flower cluster with the outer flowers opening first.

Head—a crowded cluster of stalkless (or nearly stalkless) flowers.

5

SCHEMATICS

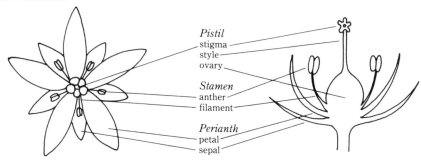

COMPLETE, REGULAR FLOWER

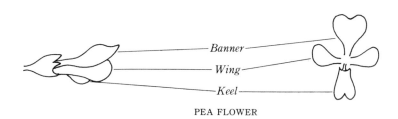

PEA FLOWER

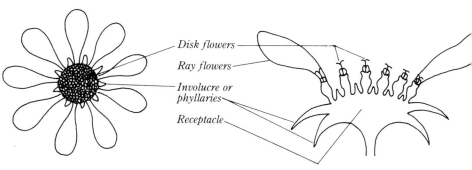

ASTER INFLORESCENCE

6

PETAL TYPES

FREE PETALS
(polypetalous)

FUSED PETALS
(sympetalous)

REGULAR
(radial symmetry)

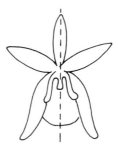

IRREGULAR
(bilateral symmetry)

Leaves

LEAF PARTS

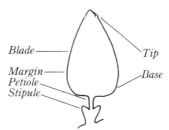

Blade ——— *Tip*

Margin ——— *Base*
Petiole
Stipule

LEAF ARRANGEMENTS

ALTERNATE   OPPOSITE   WHORLED

LEAF TYPES

SIMPLE   PALMATELY COMPOUND   PALMATELY TRIFOLIOLATE   PINNATELY TRIFOLIOLATE

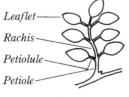  

Leaflet —
Rachis —
Petiolule —
Petiole —

ODD–PINNATE   EVEN–PINNATE   BIPINNATELY COMPOUND

LEAF VENATION

PARALLEL   RETICULATE   PINNATE   ARCUATE   PALMATE

LEAF SHAPES

LINEAR   OBLONG   OVAL

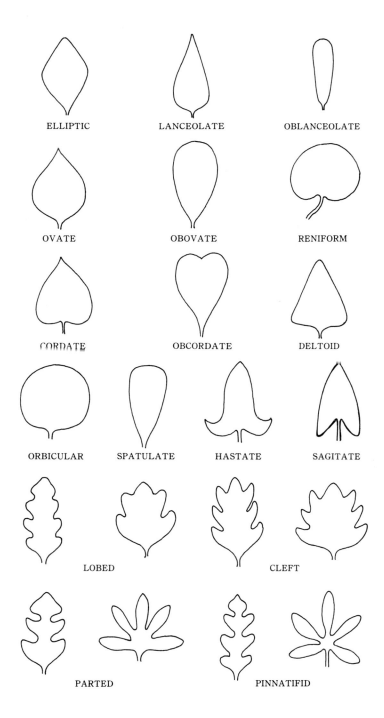

ELLIPTIC

LANCEOLATE

OBLANCEOLATE

OVATE

OBOVATE

RENIFORM

CORDATE

OBCORDATE

DELTOID

ORBICULAR

SPATULATE

HASTATE

SAGITATE

LOBED

CLEFT

PARTED

PINNATIFID

9

LEAF MARGINS

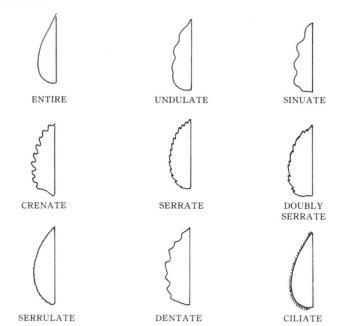

ENTIRE   UNDULATE   SINUATE

CRENATE   SERRATE   DOUBLY SERRATE

SERRULATE   DENTATE   CILIATE

Stems

AERIAL TYPES

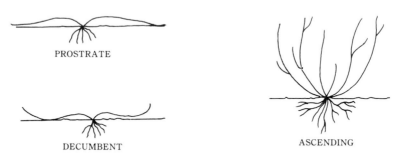

PROSTRATE

DECUMBENT

ASCENDING

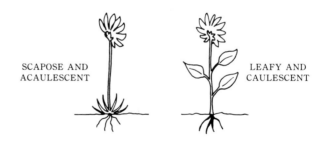

SCAPOSE AND
ACAULESCENT

LEAFY AND
CAULESCENT

REPRODUCTIVE TYPES

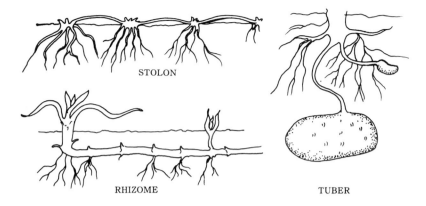

STOLON

RHIZOME

TUBER

Roots

TYPES

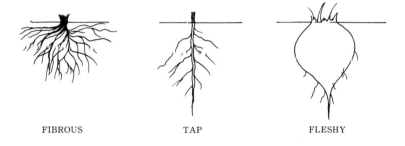

FIBROUS

TAP

FLESHY

USE OF THE KEYS

The keys in this book are designed to narrow the choices within a given flower color to a relatively few plants, with the final identification based on the plant description and color photos. Easily determined characteristics are used.

To use the keys the reader selects either 1a or 1b at the same indentation from the margin. Further choices are made from choices successively indented under the previous choice until the selected key component is followed by page numbers, which represent plants with the characters of your collected plant. The final choice is made by comparing the photos and descriptions of the plants. If the reader is uncertain as to a choice, then the plant should be keyed using both choices.

The first separation deals with fused or free flower petals. If not obvious, the reader should pull an individual petal from the flower. If the petals come off separately, then take the free petal choice. If they come out together, take the fused choice. For members of the composite family, it may appear that a single petal is removed, but actually several fused petals are being removed; so for composites (sunflower-like heads), take the fused-petal choice.

Using the basic floral and vegetative information given on preceding pages, follow a stepwise progression through the key until several page numbers are given. Again, composites offer a difficulty since both regular and irregular corollas exist in the same head. For uniformity, use the regular corolla choice for all composites.

In many instances flower color distinctions may be obscure, particularly between blue and lavender-violet or purple flowers. Many have been cross-referenced between keys, but you may need to try a different flower color key for plants that grade between the color distinctions made for this book.

K E Y / *White Flowers*

1a. Flowers with free petals (polypetalous)
  2a. Regular corolla (radial symmetry)
    3a. Alternate or basal leaves
      4a. Simple leaves
        5a. Margin entire
          6a. Leaves mostly basal, 70, 74, 76
          6b. Leaves mostly not basal
            7a. Leaves linear, 44, 72
            7b. Leaves not linear, 37, 42, 44, 45, 57
        5b. Margin not entire
          6a. Lobed, 28, 57
          6b. Toothed
            7a. Shrubs, 36, 68
            7b. Herbs, 43, 57
          6c. Pinnatifid, 57
          6d. Cleft, 22, 35, 102
      4b. Compound leaves, 40, 47
    3b. Opposite leaves
      4a. Simple leaves, 25, 27, 44, 214
      4b. Pinnately compound, 69
    3c. Whorled leaves, 29
  2b. Irregular corolla (bilateral symmetry)
    3a. Simple leaves, 64
    3b. Pinnately compound leaves
      4a. Pea flowers, 31, 32, 38, 50, 55
      4b. Not pea flowers, 60, 62, 63
    3c. Palmately compound leaves, 33, 39
1b. Flowers with fused petals (sympetalous)
  2a. Alternate leaves
    3a. Margin entire
      4a. Flowers in a head, 23, 30, 34, 41, 56
      4b. Flowers not in a head, 49, 58, 66
    3b. Margin not entire
      4a. Lobed, 53, 71
      4b. Toothed, 34, 41, 54, 73
      4c. Pinnatifid, 20
      4d. Wavy-lobed, 89
  2b. Opposite leaves
    3a. Margin entire, 52, 66
    3b. Margin toothed, 59

◄ Western Yarrow

Achillea millefolium L. ssp. *lanulosa* (Nutt.) Piper

(COMPOSITE FAMILY)

Western yarrow is an aromatic, rhizomatous perennial 1–2 ft tall with erect wooly-villous stems. Leaves are alternate and highly pinnately dissected. Basal leaves are petiolate, the upper ones cauline-sessile, with the blade 2–4 in. long and ½–1 in. wide. The composite-type heads are numerous, arranged in a flattopped inflorescence. Each head is about ¼ in. across with 5 white (sometimes pink) ray florets about ⅛ in. long. Disk florets are relatively few (10 to 30). The fruit is a small flattened achene.

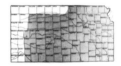

Western yarrow has a spicy aroma and has numerous purported medicinal properties. Its name comes from Achilles, who used the plant to heal wounds of his warriors. Leaves of this plant were used as a poultice for spider bites. Among the common ailments for which western yarrow has been used are influenza, gout, urinary disorders, indigestion, wounds, and a variety of others. It produces an off-flavor in milk when grazed by dairy cattle. Western yarrow has an alkaloidal poison and care should be taken in its use.

APRIL–MAY

◄ Carolina Anemone

Anemone caroliniana Walt.

(BUTTERCUP FAMILY)

Carolina anemone is a short perennial 4–8 in. tall arising from a bulbous rhizome with a single glabrous stem. The basal leaves are deeply 3-parted with short petioles. Two sessile, 3-parted leaves form an involucre subtending a single flower. The flower, which resembles superficially a composite type, has no petals but 6 to 20 narrow sepals ½–¾ in. long which vary

from white to pink to blue to violet. Numerous stamens and pistils are clustered on a convex receptacle forming a buttonlike yellowish knob. The fruit is a wooly, entangled achene.

The flowers remain closed from early to midmorning until midafternoon. Carolina anemone is often found in diffuse colonies with flowers of different colors in close proximity.

MAY–JUNE

Field Pussytoes ▶

Antennaria neglecta Greene

(COMPOSITE FAMILY)

Field pussytoes is a perennial wooly herb with sparsely leafy stolons. Leaves are ovate, alternate, and the conspicuous ones basal, ¼–½ in. wide. The stolons often develop terminal rosettes of leaves similar to the basal leaves, which are green and almost glabrous on top and whitish-wooly below. The upright stems are seldom more than 6 in. tall and have wooly, linear, cauline leaves. The plants are dioecious, with male and female flowers being borne on separate plants. The male plants are reduced in size and rare in occurrence. Female plants can develop seeds without fertilization (apomictic). Female heads are several in a clustered hemispherical whitish inflorescence. Field pussytoes is found in matlike patches and usually plants of one patch are of one sex.

The gum of the stems has been used as a chewing gum, reportedly quite nourishing.

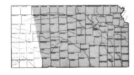

15

JUNE–AUGUST

Hemp Dogbane ▶

Apocynum cannabinum L.

(DOGBANE FAMILY)

Hemp dogbane is an erect perennial 3–4 ft tall, branched above, with milky juice. The opposite leaves are entire, ovate to lanceolate, and glabrous or pubescent beneath. The inflorescence is a branched terminal cyme of small white to greenish-white flowers. The 5 petals are fused into a bell-shaped corolla with 5 erect lobes. The fruit is a slender follicle with tufted seeds.

Though hemp dogbane is highly poisonous, losses from livestock eating it are rare because it is highly unpalatable. The fibers of this plant were used by American Indians for cord, thread, and weaving. The plant has also been used medicinally as a diuretic and heart stimulant. A decoction from the roots has been used to treat intestinal worm problems; smoke inhaled from a burning root has been used for headaches.

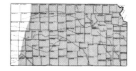

JUNE–JULY

◀ Texas Sandwort

Arenaria stricta Michx. ssp. *texana* (Robins.) Maguire

(PINK FAMILY)

Texas sandwort is a loosely tufted, erect perennial ½–1 ft tall with glabrous stems and leaves. Flowering stems have linear, opposite primary leaves ¼–¾ in. long with short, leafy, sterile shoots fascicled in their axils. The inflorescence is a moderately dense cyme. Flowers, 3 to 30 in number, have 5 white petals about ¼–½ in. long. The fruit is a 3-valved, dehiscent capsule.

Texas sandwort is found almost exclusively on rocky sites.

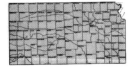

◀ **White Pricklypoppy**

Argemone polyanthemos (Fedde) G. Ownbey

(POPPY FAMILY)

White pricklypoppy is an erect annual with spiny stems, leaves, and sepals. The spiny, round stem is 2–4 ft tall and has a bluish-green color. The alternate leaves clasp the stem, with the lower ones deeply lobed and parted and the upper ones less so. The leaf margins are crisped and spiny-toothed. The flowers are solitary or in loose cymes with 4 to 6 thin, delicate petals 1–2 in. long and ¾–1 in. wide. The dense cluster of bright yellow stamens is striking. The fruit is a spiny capsule, which opens by terminal splits, with black-brown seeds.

In Kansas, white pricklypoppy is usually associated with some sort of disturbed site. The bright yellow sap of the plant offers an additional identification tool. Other species of this genus have been used to treat eye and lung diseases.

◀ **Whorled Milkweed**

Asclepias verticillata L.

(MILKWEED FAMILY)

Whorled milkweed is a slender, upright perennial 1–2½ ft tall growing from a fibrous root system. The leaves are narrowly linear, 1–3 in. long and ⅛ in. wide in whorls of 3 to 6 at each node, with an entire margin. The inflorescence consists of several umbels of small whitish flowers from the upper nodes. The petals and hoods are white or whitish-green. The pods are slender and erect, 2–3 in. long.

This plant is delicate in nature and often occurs in colonies. Livestock may be poisoned by eating it.

17

◄ Heath Aster

Aster ericoides L.

(COMPOSITE FAMILY)

Heath aster is a rhizomatous perennial with highly branched, slender stems 1–2 ft tall which may be erect or somewhat prostrate. The stem and leaves are covered with short hairs. The alternate leaves of the primary stems are linear and sessile, ¾–1 in. long. Short axillary stem branches with small linear leaves appear as the plant matures. The inflorescence is a panicle with clusters of many flowers appearing racemose. The ray florets of the small composite head (¼ in. across) are usually white, but may be pink-tinged. The anthers of the disk florets give the disk a yellow color. The fruit is a small, silky achene.

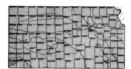

JULY–AUGUST

◄ Canada Milkvetch

Astragalus canadensis L.

(PEA FAMILY)

Canada milkvetch is an erect, glabrous to thinly hairy perennial 2–4 ft tall. The pinnately compound leaves have 13 to 20 oblong leaflets, glabrous above and sparsely hairy beneath. The inflorescence is a many-flowered raceme borne on long peduncles with creamy-white to greenish-white pea flowers. The legumes, borne in racemes, are plump and pointed.

The seeds rattle in mature pods of this plant, giving rise to the common name rattleweed or rattlebox. The leaves tend to orient themselves in an east-west plane, emulating compass-plant to a degree.

◄ Creamy Poisonvetch

Astragalus racemosus Pursh

(PEA FAMILY)

Creamy poisonvetch is an erect perennial 1–3 ft tall. Stems, glabrous or with short appressed hairs, are few and grow from a stout, thickened base. The alternate leaves are pinnately compound with 15 to 25 narrowly oblong leaflets, glabrous above and minutely hairy beneath. The inflorescence is a dense terminal raceme, cylindric in shape, of creamy-white pea flowers. The legume is upright, sessile, and thick cylindric.

Creamy poisonvetch (often called racemose loco) is found only in selenium-bearing soils and accumulates selenium in amounts toxic to livestock. Selenium poisoning has been called "blind staggers" or "alkalid disease."

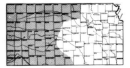

◄ Atlantic Wildindigo

Baptisia leucantha T. & G.

(PEA FAMILY)

Atlantic wildindigo is an upright, glabrous, stout perennial 2–4 ft tall. The alternate leaves are palmately trifoliolate with oblanceolate leaflets. The inflorescence is a terminal, upright raceme of large creamy-white pea flowers. The legume is ellipsoid, 1–2 in. long, tapering into a conspicuous beak, and turning black on ripening.

The young growth of all species of wildindigo resembles asparagus but must not be eaten since poisoning will occur.

19

◄ **Tuberous Indianplantain**

Cacalia tuberosa Nutt.

(COMPOSITE FAMILY)

Tuberous indianplantain is an erect, glabrous perennial 2–5 ft tall arising from a short, tuberous-thickened base and fleshy, fibrous roots. The alternate ovate leaves are thick and firm and may be slightly toothed. Several prominent parallel veins converge toward the summit of the leaf blade. The flat-topped inflorescence is composed of white flower heads with 5 tubular disk florets. The corolla is deeply 5-cleft. The fruit is an oblong achene with a silky pappus.

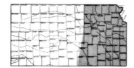

MAY–JUNE

◄ **Pale Poppymallow**

Callirhoe alcaeoides (Michx.) Gray

(MALLOW FAMILY)

Pale poppymallow is an erect perennial 5–15 in. tall arising from a thickened root. The alternate leaves with hairy petioles are suborbicular, 1–1½ in. in diameter, and coarsely crenate to palmately lobed. Basal leaves are sometimes triangular-shaped and incised. The flowers are white to pinkish, 1 to a flower stalk, and with 5 free petals that overlap somewhat and are erose or notched on the tip. The fruit is of separate carpels, rugose and glabrous on the back.

Like purple poppymallow, the root of this plant can be eaten raw or cooked.

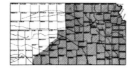

◄ **Inland Ceanothus**

Ceanothus herbaceus Rat. var. *pubescens* (T. & G.) Shinners

(BUCKTHORN FAMILY)

Inland ceanothus is a bushy shrub 2–3 ft tall with alternate oblong to elliptic leaves whose margin is glandular-serrate. The inflorescence is an umbellate panicle of white, 5-petaled flowers. The petals are long-clawed and narrow, forming a cup. The fruit is a 3-lobed black capsule.

The leaves and flowers are used to make a tea for treating fevers, dysentery, and sore mouth and throat. The flowers lather when crushed and rubbed in water and are said to leave the skin soft and fragrant.

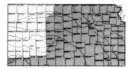

MAY–JULY

◄ **Pale Comandra**

Comandra umbellata (L.) Nutt. ssp. *pallida* (A. DC.) M. E. Jones

(SANDALWOOD FAMILY)

Pale comandra is an erect, glabrous perennial 4–8 in. tall arising from a stout rhizome. The roots are at least partially parasitic on roots of other plants. The alternate entire leaves are small, linear to lanceolate, with a thick, leathery texture. The greenish to cream flowers are borne in terminal axillary clusters of 3 to 5. Each flower has 5 petals and 5 sepals with the hypanthium wholly or partly enclosing the inferior ovary, forming an urn-shaped false fruit.

Pale comandra (sometimes called bastard toadflax) has green leaves and though parasitic is capable of supporting itself. The fruit can be eaten raw.

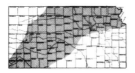

21

Nineanther Dalea ▶

Dalea enneandra Nutt.

(PEA FAMILY)

Nineanther dalea is an erect, glabrous perennial 1–3 ft tall arising from a taproot. The alternate leaves are pinnately compound with 5 to 11 glandular-dotted, linear leaflets. The inflorescence is of several loosely flowered spikes with white (sometimes lavender) pea flowers with 9 stamens. The fruit is a 1-seeded legume enclosed in a persistent calyx.

The large taproot of this species is yellow in the ground but turns orange when exposed to the air and sunlight.

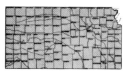

◀ Plains Larkspur

Delphinium virescens Nutt.

(CROWFOOT FAMILY)

Plains larkspur is an erect perennial 1–3½ ft tall growing from a woody rootstock. The plant is finely and abundantly pubescent throughout. The alternate leaves are mostly basal, 2–5 in. wide, and palmately divided. The inflorescence is a terminal raceme of creamy-white flowers tinged with a bluish-purple spot. The flower is composed of 5 petallike sepals, the uppermost prolonged into a spur, and 4 petals, the lower 2 bifid and bearded or gnawed. The fruit is a cylindric follicle with small brown seeds densely covered with projecting scales.

This plant contains the alkaloidal poison delphinine, as do most larkspurs, and is poisonous to livestock, particularly cattle.

◀ **Illinois Bundleflower**

Desmanthus illinoensis (Michx.) MacM.

(PEA FAMILY)

Illinois bundleflower is an erect, essentially glabrous perennial 2–4 ft tall with a strongly angled stem (longitudinally grooved). The alternate leaves are bipinnately compound with 6 to 12 pairs of pinnae, each with 20 to 30 pairs of leaflets. The leaves are touch-sensitive and infold in strong sunlight or on being handled. The leaf petiole has 1 or more glands. The regular flowers are composed of 5 united sepals and 5 free petals, white to whitish-green in color. The perianth is inconspicuous since the globose head is overtopped by the white stamens (5 per flower). The fruit is a lunar-shaped flat legume in a globose head of many.

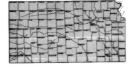

MAY–JUNE

Daisy Fleabane ▶

Erigeron strigosus Muhl.

(COMPOSITE FAMILY)

Daisy fleabane is an erect, branched annual (rarely biennial) 1–2 ft tall with spreading hairs. The basal leaves are oblanceolate to spatulate, entire or toothed near the apex. The upper leaves are alternate, linear to lanceolate, and moderately hairy. The inflorescence is flattopped, composed of small heads with numerous white rays (sometimes pinkish or bluish) and yellow head florets. The fruit is a slender achene with a bristly pappus.

Fleabane derives its common name from the early European belief that members of this genus would keep fleas away.

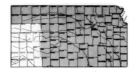

23

JULY–SEPTEMBER
◄ Annual Eriogonum

Eriogonum annuum Nutt.

(BUCKWHEAT FAMILY)

Annual eriogonum is an erect annual, unbranched to the inflorescence. The leaves and stem are covered with floccose, silky hairs (cobwebby). The oblong to lanceolate leaves are arranged alternately above and clustered below. The inflorescence is a flattopped cyme with small white flowers of 6 sepals; several flowers are clustered above a bell-shaped involucre. The fruit is a 3-angled achene, globular at the base and beaked.

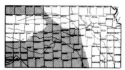

JULY–SEPTEMBER
◄ Buttonsnakeroot Eryngo

Eryngium yuccifolium Michx.

(PARSLEY FAMILY)

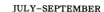

Buttonsnakeroot eryngo is an erect perennial 3–5 ft tall. The solitary stem has alternate linear-lanceolate leaves with parallel venation and weak spines on the margin. The leaf bases clasp the stem. The umbellate head is round-ovoid with small flowers exceeded by whitish bracts.

The leaf of this plant resembles *Yucca,* giving rise to the specific epithet. While the head resembles a thistle, it is an umbel of the carrot family. The roots have been used as an emetic, expectorant, and diaphoretic.

Flowering Spurge
Euphorbia corollata L.
(SPURGE FAMILY)

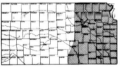

Flowering spurge is an erect perennial 1–3 ft tall with slender, glabrous to villous stems. The stem leaves are alternate, linear to linear-oblong, and sessile. The leaves subtending the inflorescence are similar, but whorled. The leaves of the inflorescence are smaller and opposite or alternate. The inflorescence is a flattopped to paniculate cyme. The showy part of the white flowers is a cup-shaped, 5-parted involucre containing the small inconspicuous true flower. The fruit is a broad capsule which breaks open with enough force to send the seed a considerable distance.

Flowering spurge is a poisonous plant but is seldom eaten by livestock. The milky juice can cause skin irritation. Occasionally used as a medicine, it sometimes causes bad side effects.

25

◄ Snow-on-the-Mountain

Euphorbia marginata Pursh

(SPURGE FAMILY)

Snow-on-the-mountain is an erect annual, branched above, 2–4 ft tall. The plant is softly villous, especially above, with stems reddish toward the base. The alternate stem leaves are sessile, entire, and broadly ovate to elliptic or obovate-oblong. The leaves subtending the inflorescence are whorled to opposite. The inflorescence is a crowded cyme with the subtending leaves white-margined or entirely white. The involucre has 5 white petallike bracts. The conspicuous ovary is green and 3-lobed.

Though not a milkweed, snow-on-the-mountain has milky juice which produces inflammation of the skin. So strong is the irritation that it has been used to brand cattle in Texas. When eaten by livestock, poisoning occurs. Snow-on-the-mountain also accumulates selenium if that element is in the soil, which also causes toxicity to livestock.

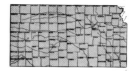

◄ Wild Strawberry

Fragaria virginiana Duchn. var. *illinoensis* (Prince) Gray

(ROSE FAMILY)

Wild strawberry is a trailing perennial 4–8 in. tall, which is spread by stolons (runners). The trifoliolately compound leaves are basal, with petiolules, ovate to obovate leaflets, and toothed on the margin. The lower leaf surface is pubescent with a whitish bloom, the upper surface glabrous to sparsely pubescent. The inflorescence has a few to several white flowers borne on scape-like peduncles. The flowers have 5 white free petals and numerous conspicuous yellow stamens. The fruit is a red, ovoid, enlarged receptacle bearing small achenes in pits on the surface.

This plant can have bisexual and unisexual flowers on different plants.

Among the many prairie wildflowers, this plant ranks at the top as an edible. The juicy, tangy fruits are a treat to the palate. They can be eaten raw or used as cultivated strawberries are—for jelly or jam. The American Indians used the green leaves for a delicious tea. Many medicinal properties have been claimed for the leaves of this plant. Among its varied uses are as a tonic, as a mild astringent, and to alkalize the system. The fruit is purported to tighten loose teeth, clear blurred vision, clean teeth, and remedy gout. The juice rubbed on the skin has been used to clear up spots.

JULY–SEPTEMBER

Field Snakecotton ►

Froelichia floridana (Nutt.) Moq. var. *campestris* (Small) Fern.

(AMARANTH FAMILY)

Field snakecotton is an erect, slender annual 2–3 ft tall with puberulent to lanate stems. The narrow opposite leaves are oblong-linear to narrowly spatulate, canescent above, thinly tomentose below, and attenuate at the base. The inflorescence is a terminal, bracted spike with a tubular, united, 5-parted calyx. Petals are absent. The entire inflorescence is white and densely wooly. The fruit is a 1-seeded, unopening utricle.

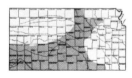

◄ American Licorice

Glycyrrhiza lepidota Pursh

(PEA FAMILY)

American licorice is an erect, glabrous perennial 1–3 ft tall. The alternate leaves are pinnately compound with 11 to 19 oblong or lanceolate leaflets, glandular-dotted below. The inflorescence is made up of axillary racemes of white to greenish-white pea flowers. The fruit is ellipsoid, indehiscent, and covered with hooked prickles, turning reddish-brown at maturity.

The fruits of this plant resemble cockleburs and are admirably adapted for seed dispersal in that they readily cling to passersby. The genus name means sweet root and the root, when eaten or chewed raw, has a distinct flavor. According to one author, American licorice is in no way inferior to the Old World cultivated licorice which contains considerable quantities of flavorings, sugars, and compounds used in medicine, candy, root beer, and chewing tobacco. Among the many purported medicinal properties are uses as a purgative; to treat inflamed membranes of the nose and throat, toothache, and earache; as a uterine cleanser; and for blood clotting.

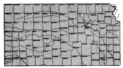

JUNE–AUGUST

◄ Narrowleaf Bluets

Hedyotis nigricans (Lam.) Fosb.

(BEDSTRAW FAMILY)

Narrowleaf bluets is an erect perennial 6–18 in. tall with numerous stems arising from a single base. The stems are glabrous or somewhat pubescent below. The opposite leaves are linear and sessile, with small axillary leaves in a cluster giving the appearance of a whorled arrangement. The inflorescence is a crowded panicle of small white (sometimes pink-tinged) salverform flowers of 4 fused petals. The fruit is an obovoid capsule.

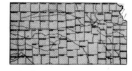

Flattop Hymenopappus ▶

Hymenopappus scabiosaeus L'Her. var. *corymbosus*
(T. & G.) B. L. Turner

(COMPOSITE FAMILY)

Flattop hymenopappus is an erect biennial 2–4 ft tall with wooly, ribbed stems. The alternate leaves are broadly lanceolate, pinnately parted, and reduced above. The basal rosette leaves often are not lobed. The stem does not elongate until the second season of growth. The rayless heads are clustered into a flattopped inflorescence with white to creamy-white disk florets. The involucral bracts are loose and broad, the upper part petallike and white. The achene has minute pappus scales.

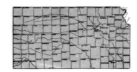

◀ Falseboneset

Kuhnia eupatorioides L. var. *corymbulosa* T. & G.

(COMPOSITE FAMILY)

Falseboneset is an erect perennial 1–2 ft tall, densely puberulent to subglabrous. The alternate leaves are narrowly lanceolate to broadly rhombic-lanceolate with gold-colored glandular dots beneath. Heads are rayless and form flattopped clusters at the ends of the branches. The corolla of the disk flowers is creamy white. The plumose pappus of the achene is striking.

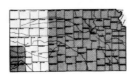

29

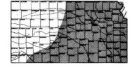

◄ Roundhead Lespedeza

Lespedeza capitata Michx.

(PEA FAMILY)

Roundhead lespedeza is an erect perennial 2–5 ft tall with a sparsely to densely silvery-pubescent stem. The alternate leaves are pinnately trifoliolate, subsessile, and with awl-shaped stipules. The leaflets are oblong-lanceolate to mostly elliptic and are nearly glabrous above but densely silvery-pubescent below. The inflorescence is a globose clustered head of small cream to white pea flowers. The adherent calyx is reddish-brown and persists throughout the dormant season atop the stem. The legume is a small, oblong, densely pubescent pod.

This plant is useful in dry arrangements because of the persistent calyx. The Comanche Indians made a beverage from the leaves.

JUNE–JULY

◄ Babywhite Aster

Leucelene ericoides (Torr.) Greene

(COMPOSITE FAMILY)

Babywhite aster is an erect perennial 2–6 in. tall growing from a woody branching caudex or creeping rhizomes. The stems are numerous, tufted, often glandular, and bristly hairy. The alternate leaves are simple, rarely over ¼ in. long, linear to linear-oblanceolate, hispid-ciliate, and entire. The heads are solitary on slender branches with short white rays and a yellow disk. The fruit is an achene with appressed hairs and a copious pappus.

30

◄ White Eveningprimrose

Oenothera speciosa Nutt.

(EVENINGPRIMROSE FAMILY)

White eveningprimrose is an erect perennial 1–2 ft tall arising from a slender rhizome. The alternate leaves are oblong-lanceolate, entire to dentate-lobed to pinnatified, and glabrous to canescent. The flowers are sessile in the axils of the upper leaves, forming spicate clusters. The corolla is composed of 4 white, sometimes grading to pink, thin petals. The calyx forms a long tube extending to the inferior ovary. The stigma is large and 4-lobed. The fruit is a winged capsule ¼–½ in. long.

The flowers open toward evening and close during the warm part of the day. The plants are usually found in large colonies, particularly in disturbed areas such as roadside ditches.

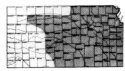

JUNE–JULY

◄ Western Marbleseed

Onosmodium molle Michx. var. *occidentale* (Mock.) I. M. Johnst.

(BORAGE FAMILY)

Western marbleseed is an erect, clustered perennial 1–3 ft tall, roughly grayish-pubescent throughout. The alternate leaves are ovate-lanceolate to lanceolate, sessile, and strongly veined. The inflorescence is a terminal, bracteose spike with 5 regular, fused, white to creamy to greenish petals. The 5 lobes of the corolla converge at the summits. The plant completes its reproduction function prior to the opening of the corolla. The nutlets are white and shiny and extremely hard, giving rise to the name marbleseed.

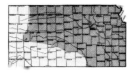

31

White Penstemon ►

Penstemon albidus Nutt.

(SNAPDRAGON FAMILY)

White penstemon is an erect perennial 1–2 ft tall, finely pubescent throughout. The opposite sessile leaves are oblong-lanceolate, entire or sparsely toothed, and ascending and clasp the stem to a degree. The inflorescence is a terminal racemelike cluster with numerous linear, bracted leaves. The tubular white flowers are 5-lobed, trumpet-shaped, and bilabiate. The corolla is covered with capitate, glandular hairs. Of the 5 stamens, 4 are functional and 1 is represented only by a bearded filament (staminode), hence the oft-applied common name, beardtongue. The fruit is a small capsule.

◄ White Prairieclover

Petalostemon candidum (Willd.) Michx.

(PEA FAMILY)

White prairieclover is an erect perennial 1–2 ft tall with simple or sparingly branched glabrous stems. The alternate leaves are pinnately compound with 5 to 9 linear to oblong leaflets. The leaflets are entire, glabrous, and glandular-punctate beneath. The inflorescence is of 1 to few spikes with white flowers. The corolla is not pealike, but has 1 large white petal borne on a capillary claw and 4 others reduced to staminodes, also borne on capillary clawlike filaments. Each flower is subtended by a bract. The pod is a thin-walled legume enclosed in a persistent calyx.

American Indians used bruised leaves of this plant steeped in water for application to fresh wounds. They also made a tea from the leaves and chewed the roots.

◄ Roundheaded Prairieclover

Petalostemon multiflorum Nutt.

(PEA FAMILY)

Roundheaded prairieclover is a bushy, erect perennial 1–3 ft tall with glabrous stems. The alternate leaves are pinnately compound with 5 to 9 leaflets. The leaflets are linear-oblong to cuneate-oblong, glabrous, and glandular-dotted below. The inflorescence is of globose heads of white pea flowers with 5 conspicuous, long-clawed petals. Each flower is subtended by a bract. The legume is small and enclosed in a persistent calyx.

One author reports that Indians used the leaves for a tea and as a preventive medicine. The roots were chewed and the stems tied together for use as brooms.

JUNE–SEPTEMBER

◄ Roughseed Clammyweed

Polanisia dodecandra (L.) DC. ssp. *trachysperma* (T. & G.) Iltis

(CAPER FAMILY)

Roughseed clammyweed is an erect annual 1–2 ft tall, clammy-pubescent throughout. The alternate leaves are trifoliolate, with elliptic to narrowly ovate leaflets. The inflorescence is a terminal raceme of somewhat irregular flowers. The 4 petals have a narrowed, clawlike base and are white to pink. The filaments are purple and extend much above the corolla. The fruit is a slender, erect, triangular pod that splits into 2 parts.

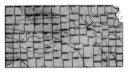

33

◀ **White Polygala**

Polygala alba Nutt.

(MILKWORT FAMILY)

White polygala is an erect perennial 6–12 in. tall with several glabrous stems arising from a single base. The alternate leaves are linear to linear-lanceolate with the margins rolled under to a degree. The inflorescence is a terminal raceme of white irregular flowers with 2 white petallike sepals and 3 small green ones. The 3 petals are fused and connected to the stamen tubes. The fruit is a small capsule with a fleshy outgrowth of the stalk of the ovule (aril) half as long as the seed.

The dried root of members of this genus has been used to treat snakebite and respiratory illnesses. The herbal term for the root of this plant is "senega." The Sioux used a decoction of the root for earache.

JULY–SEPTEMBER

◀ **Common Devilsclaw**

Proboscidea louisianica (Mill.) Thell.

(PEDALIUM FAMILY)

Common devilsclaw is a spreading annual 6–18 in. tall, densely viscid-pubescent throughout. The alternate leaves, sometimes opposite below, are suborbicular with a prominent basal sinus. The inflorescence is a terminal raceme of lavender tubular flowers, sometimes white to yellow. The bilabiate corolla has 5 lobes and is mottled with purple or yellow within. The fruit is a 2-valved capsule 4–6 in. long with a long, pointed horn. As the fleshy part falls off, the woody inner parts remain. The horn splits, forming 2 curved hooks.

The horned fruit of this plant attaches to passing animals, which makes for effective seed dispersal. The young fruits may be pickled or boiled and eaten. The seeds from the pod are tasty and have a high oil content. The plant emits a strong, unpleasant odor.

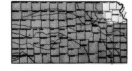

◄ Chickasaw Plum

Prunus angustifolia Marsh.

(ROSE FAMILY)

Chickasaw plum is a highly branched shrubby or treelike perennial 2–10 ft tall which forms thickets. The reddish-brown stem often has spinose branchlets. The alternate leaves are elliptic to oblanceolate, trough-shaped, smooth and shiny above, finely serrulate, and bearing a gland at the sinus of the serration. The inflorescence is composed of sessile lateral umbels of 2 to 4 flowers. The corolla has 5 white petals. The fruit is a subglobose red stonefruit.

The plums of this plant are excellent eaten raw, cooked, or dried. Delicious jam or jelly can be made as well. The flowers appear prior to leaf initiation and the fruit ripens much later, in August.

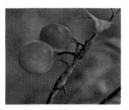

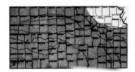

JUNE–AUGUST

◄ American Elderberry

Sambucus canadensis L.

(HONEYSUCKLE FAMILY)

American elderberry is an erect stoloniferous shrub 3–10 ft tall. The woody stems contain a large white pith. The opposite leaves are pinnately compound with 5 to 11 broadly lanceolate to ovate leaflets having sharply serrate margins. The leaflets are usually glabrous, but may be pubescent underneath. The inflorescence is a compound cyme 4–8 in. across. The flowers have 5 or 6 white petals united at the base. The fruit is a purplish-black berry.

Elderberry wine is an old favorite, but is by no means the only use for this plant. Jams, jellies, and pies can be made from the fruits. The inflorescence may also be dipped in batter and fried. The leaves, bark, and berries have been used in treating colds and wounds, breaking fevers, washing irritated eyes, and as a purgative.

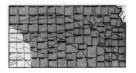

35

◄ Prairie Blue-eyedgrass

Sisyrinchium campestre Bickn. var. *campestre*

(IRIS FAMILY)

Prairie blue-eyedgrass is a low, grasslike perennial 4–10 in. tall. The leaves are mostly basal, equitant, and linear. The inflorescence is an umbel-like cluster of white to pink to blue flowers with yellow throats. The 3 sepals and 3 petals are alike and arise from a 2-bracted spathe borne on a 2-valved peduncle (scape) arising from the rootstock. The fruit is a globose capsule.

When not in flower, this plant is commonly mistaken for a grass but is a member of the lily family. Often blue, pink, and white flowers grow in close proximity.

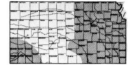

Carolina Horsenettle ►

Solanum carolinense L.

(NIGHTSHADE FAMILY)

Carolina horsenettle is a branched, erect perennial 1–2 ft tall arising from slender, creeping rhizomes. The stem is spiny, with fine, stellate pubescence. The alternate leaves are ovate, have 2 to 5 shallow lobes, and are more or less spiny on the midrib beneath. The inflorescence is a 1-sided raceme with blue, violet, or white flowers. The corolla is 5-lobed and fused and the yellow anthers are conspicuous. The fruit is a spherical yellow berry.

This plant contains an alkaloid, solanine, which has been used medicinally as a sedative and antispasmodic, primarily in the treatment of epilepsy. In colonial times the juice from 5 or 6 berries was taken daily in increasing doses to treat tetanus. The root is believed to contain a sedative.

JULY–SEPTEMBER
Stenosiphon ►

Stenosiphon linifolius (Nutt.) Heynh.

(EVENINGPRIMROSE FAMILY)

Stenosiphon is an erect perennial, simple or branched above, 2–5 ft tall, and glabrous throughout. The alternate leaves are sessile, narrowly linear-lanceolate to lanceolate, and thick and firm. The inflorescence is a many-flowered elongated spike of white flowers. The flower has 4 petals and an elongated tube (hypanthium) running downward to the ovary. The fruit is ovoid to lanceoloid, pubescent, and 4-angled.

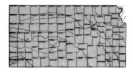

JUNE–AUGUST
◄ Moth Mullein

Verbascum blattaria L.

(SNAPDRAGON FAMILY)

Moth mullein is an erect biennial 2–4 ft tall with slender stems, glandular-pubescent above. The alternate leaves are a basal rosette during the first year, petiolate, oblong to narrowly triangular, and doubly serrate. The upper leaves are sessile, partly clasping, and ovate-lanceolate. The inflorescence is a terminal, solitary raceme of yellow, pink, or white flowers. The corolla has 5 fused petals and 5 lobes. The white corollas are tinged pinkish-purple at the throat. The fruit is an ovoid brown capsule.

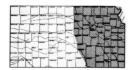

37

Small Soapweed ▶

Yucca glauca Nutt.

(LILY FAMILY)

Small soapweed is an evergreen perennial 1–3 ft tall arising from a short, large caudex. The alternate linear leaves form a basal rosette and are spine-tipped, leathery, and highly fibrous. The branching rootstock gives rise to clumps of plants. The inflorescence is a raceme of drooping cup-shaped flowers borne on a stout flower stalk 2–5 ft tall. The white to greenish-white flowers have 6 similar perianth members, 3 each in 2 series. The fruit is a drooping, 6-sided, 3-valved capsule.

An interesting obligate, mutualistic relationship has developed between yucca and the yucca moth *(Pronuba)*. The moth enters a flower and proceeds to the anthers, deliberately gathering pollen with mouth parts specialized for that function, storing it under the chin. After collecting a large ball of pollen, it flies to another plant, inserts its ovipositor into the ovary of the yucca, and deposits eggs. Then the moth climbs to the stigma and spreads the pollen from another plant on the stigmatic surface, thus accomplishing cross-pollination. The pollen-laden moth visits other flowers on the same plant, as well as flowers on other plants, ovipositing and pollinating. The eggs hatch, and the larvae consume only a portion of the ovules prior to boring out and dropping to the soil where they imbed themselves to overwinter and emerge as moths when the yucca blooms, to start again this amazing cycle. Neither species can exist without the other, truly a marvelous evolutionary adaptation.

American Indians used the pounded roots as soap, hence the name soapweed. Southwest Indians called the soap "amole," and certain tribes had to wash their hair with it prior to ceremonials. They also used the fibers from the leaves for twine, baskets, sandals,

whips, and brooms. Small soapweed also provided food for them. The pulp of the near-ripe pods was eaten as were flowers, buds, and young flower stalks. The young flower stalks were boiled to make a red winelike drink which was said to make one "brave and valiant." Further simmering made a syrup used for rubbing on rheumatic joints. The root was also used as a laxative.

APRIL–MAY

◄ **Nuttall Deathcamas**

Zigadenus nuttallii Gray

(LILY FAMILY)

Nuttall deathcamas is an erect perennial 1–1½ ft tall growing from a bulb. The broad grasslike leaves form a basal rosette and are folded along the midrib. The stem and basal leaves recurve. The inflorescence is a simple, terminal raceme of white flowers. The 6 similar perianth parts are in 2 rows of 3 each. The fruit is an ovoid 3-valved capsule.

This plant is highly poisonous and occasional livestock losses occur, primarily from livestock eating the new growth which may be the only appreciable green growth available at that time of year. Human poisoning has occurred from mistaking the bulbs for wild onion or hyacinth.

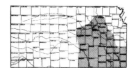

39

K E Y / *Blue Flowers*

1a. Flowers with free petals (polypetalous)
  2a. Regular corolla (radial symmetry)
    3a. Margin entire, 70, 90
    3b. Margin not entire, 22
  2b. Irregular corolla (bilateral symmetry)
    3a. Alternate or basal leaves
      4a. Simple leaves, 124
      4b. Compound leaves
        5a. Pinnately compound, 78, 79
        5b. Palmately or digitately compound
          6a. Leaves glabrous, 81
          6b. Leaves with hairs
            7a. Leaves silvery-silky pubescent, 82
            7b. Leaves not silvery-silky pubescent, 83, 84, 85, 86
    3b. Opposite leaves, 121
1b. Flowers with fused petals (sympetalous)
  2a. Regular corolla (radial symmetry)
    3a. Alternate leaves
      4a. Margin entire, 80, 89, 93
      4b. Margin not entire, 71, 102
    3b. Opposite leaves, 105
  2b. Irregular corolla (bilateral symmetry), 87, 88, 119

JUNE–JULY

◄ **Leadplant**

Amorpha canescens Pursh

(PEA FAMILY)

Leadplant is a low perennial shrub, canescent throughout, with erect stems. The alternate leaves are pinnately compound with the leaflets of an odd number (15 to 51) and small in size, ¼–½ in. long. The inflorescence is a crowded raceme 2–4 in. long. The blue flowers show only a single small petal with bright yellow to yellowish-orange conspicuous anthers. The fruit is a small legume about ⅛ in. long.

American Indians used the dried leaves for tea and pipe smoking. They also cut small pieces of the stem and attached one end to the skin by moistening it; they then burned the stem down to the skin to ward off neuralgia and rheumatism.

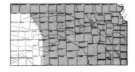

MAY–JUNE

◄ **Indigobush Amorpha**

Amorpha fruticosa L.

(PEA FAMILY)

Indigobush amorpha is a tall, bushy, perennial shrub, sparsely pubescent to glabrous, which grows up to 12 ft in height. The alternate leaves are pinnately compound with 11 to 25 leaflets ¾–1½ in. long. The inflorescence consists of 2 to several racemes 2–5 in. long. The flower is represented by a single blue to violet petal with conspicuous yellow to yellowish-orange anthers. The fruit is a glandular-dotted legume ¼–⅜ in. long and ⅛ in. wide with 2 seeds.

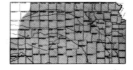

41

◄ Smooth Aster

Aster laevis L.

(COMPOSITE FAMILY)

Smooth aster is an erect, glabrous perennial 1–3 ft tall with simple to somewhat branched, slender stems arising from a short rhizome. The alternate leaves are simple, clasping the stem, lanceolate, and reduced above. The inflorescence is of numerous heads in an open panicle. The ray florets are blue to bluish-purple and the disk yellow. The fruit is a glabrous achene.

Smoke from burning the entire plant has been used to treat fainting and comas.

MAY–JUNE

◄ Blue Wildindigo

Baptisia australis (L.) R. Br. var. *minor* (Lehn.) Fern.

(PEA FAMILY)

Blue wildindigo is an erect, solitary perennial 1½–3 ft tall, glabrous throughout. The leaves are palmately trifoliolate with oblong leaflets and moderate lanceolate stipules. The inflorescence is an erect, terminal raceme with large blue pea flowers. The legume is 1–3 in. long, ellipsoid, with a beaked tip. The pods turn purplish-black at maturity.

The pods rattle profusely when mature, due to the loose seeds inside, but seeds are seldom found in the pods since insect predation is almost universal.

JUNE–JULY
◄ Silverleaf Scurfpea

Psoralea argophylla Pursh

(PEA FAMILY)

Silverleaf scurfpea is a highly branched, erect perennial 1–2 ft tall, silvery silky–white throughout, growing from rhizomes. The leaves are palmately trifoliolate with elliptic-lanceolate to oblanceolate leaflets. The inflorescence is a dense spike of purple to blue-purple pea flowers. The small legume is ovoid and silky.

Poisoning of a child who ate the seeds of this plant has been reported. However, it has been used medicinally to treat wounds; the roots have been used as a mild stimulant.

MAY–JUNE
Tallbread Scurfpea ►

Psoralea cuspidata Pursh

(PEA FAMILY)

Tallbread scurfpea is an erect to semidecumbent perennial 6–18 in. tall with a highly branched, glabrous stem. The alternate leaves are digitately compound with 5 narrowly obovate or oblong-obovate, glandular-punctate leaflets. The leaflets are glabrous above and strigose below. The inflorescence is a short, dense raceme of fairly large blue to blue-purple pea flowers. The fruit is a glandular short-beaked legume.

The root of this plant may be peeled and eaten raw or cooked. It may also be dried and ground as flour.

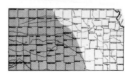

43

◀ **Common Breadroot Scurfpea**

Psoralea esculenta Pursh

(PEA FAMILY)

Common breadroot scurfpea is an erect perennial 6–12 in. tall arising from a tuberous root; it is pilose throughout. The alternate leaves are digitately compound with 5 oblong to narrowly obovate leaflets. The inflorescence is a dense spike of blue pea flowers sometimes tinged white. The fruit is a small hairy legume.

The starchy root of this plant has been called Indian turnip because of its taste and use as food. The root may be cooked or eaten raw.

◀ **Manyflower Scurfpea**

Psoralea tenuiflora Pursh var. *floribunda* (Nutt.) Rydb.

(PEA FAMILY)

Manyflower scurfpea is an erect, highly branched perennial 1–3 ft tall with a grayish-pubescent stem. The alternate leaves are digitately compound with 3 to 5 narrowly elliptic to oblanceolate, glandular-dotted leaflets. The inflorescence is an axillary raceme of numerous small blue to lavender pea flowers. The fruit is a small glandular-dotted legume with 1 seed.

Slimflower Scurfpea ►

Psoralea tenuiflora Pursh var. *tenuiflora*

(PEA FAMILY)

Slimflower scurfpea is an erect, highly branched perennial 1–3 ft tall with a grayish-pubescent stem. The alternate leaves are digitately compound with 3 to 5 narrowly elliptic to oblanceolate, glandular-dotted leaflets. The inflorescence is an axillary raceme of a few small blue to lavender pea flowers. The fruit is a glandular-dotted, 1-seeded legume.

Slimflower scurfpea and manyflower scurfpea are very similar but grow in different areas of Kansas. They may be differentiated by the number of flowers; also, the copiously pubescent calyx of manyflower scurfpea differs from the appressed-pubescent calyx of slimflower.

◄ Fringeleaf Ruellia

Ruellia humilis Nutt.

(ACANTHUS FAMILY)

Fringeleaf ruellia is an erect, simple or branched perennial 6–12 in. tall with slender, hairy stems. The opposite leaves are oblong to oblong-lanceolate, sessile, and with stiff hairs on the leaf margin (fringed). The tubular blue to blue-purple flowers are borne in the upper leaf axils. The tubular 5-lobed corolla is trumpet-shaped and readily falls when handled. The fruit is a small glabrous capsule.

45

◄ **Pitcher Sage**

Salvia pitcheri Torr.

(MINT FAMILY)

Pitcher sage is an erect perennial 2–4 ft tall with a minutely pubescent square stem with retrorse hairs. The opposite leaves are linear to lanceolate and sharply serrate on the margin. The younger leaves have internal glands that secrete an offensive odor unlike that of other sages. The inflorescence is a raceme of azure-blue flowers. The corolla is 2-lipped and falls off readily when the plant is handled. The fruit is composed of 4 single-seeded nutlets.

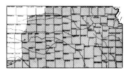

MAY–AUGUST

Silverleaf Nightshade ►

Solanum elaeagnifolium Cav.

(NIGHTSHADE FAMILY)

Silverleaf nightshade is an erect, sparsely spiny perennial 1–2 ft tall, silvery-pubescent throughout. The alternate leaves are linear to oblong to oblong-lanceolate and entire to sinuate. The inflorescence is an axillary cyme of blue, violet, or white flowers. The 5-lobed corolla has 5 fused petals; the yellow anthers are conspicuous. The fruit is a spherical yellow berry.

As with Carolina horsenettle, this plant is highly poisonous and has similar medicinal properties. The Pima and Zuni Indians used berries from this plant to curdle goat's milk.

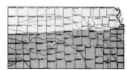

46

◄ **Spiderwort**

Tradescantia ohiensis Raf.

(SPIDERWORT FAMILY)

Spiderwort is an erect, glabrous perennial with mucilaginous sap. The alternate sessile leaves are long and narrowly linear, often with a whitish bloom. The inflorescence is a terminal umbellike cyme subtended by reflexed, leafy bracts. The flowers are 3-merous, with 3 green sepals and 3 blue to rose petals. The fruit is a 3-celled capsule.

One colorful common name, "cowslobbers," has been given this plant because of the strings of mucilaginous sap.

47

K E Y / *Lavender, Violet, and Purple Flowers*

1a. Flowers with free petals (polypetalous)
  2a. Regular corolla (radial symmetry)
    3a. Simple leaves, 22, 90, 97, 102, 124
    3b. Compound leaves, 112
  2b. Irregular corolla (bilateral symmetry)
    3a. Pinnately compound leaves
      4a. Pealike flowers
        5a. Plants prostrate and viny, 123, 206
        5b. Plants not prostrate and viny
          6a. Plants with hooked hairs, 185, 197
          6b. Plants without hooked hairs, 38, 95, 96, 114, 118
      4b. Flowers not pealike, 78, 79, 110, 118, 203
    3b. Palmately compound leaves, 82, 83, 85, 86
1b. Flowers with fused petals (sympetalous)
  2a. Regular corolla
    3a. Alternate leaves
      4a. Margin entire
        5a. Flowers in a head
          6a. Heads clustered, spikelike, 106, 107, 108
          6b. Heads not clustered or spikelike, 80, 93, 94
        5b. Flowers not in a head, 89, 200
      4b. Margin not entire
        5a. Lobed, 71, 98, 100, 104
        5b. Toothed, 100, 104, 122
        5c. Pinnatifid, 99, 109
    3b. Opposite leaves, 101, 103, 105, 121
  2b. Irregular corolla (bilateral symmetry)
    3a. Stem rounded, 87, 116, 117, 119, 120
    3b. Stem square, 88, 110, 207

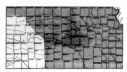

◄ **Aromatic Aster**

Aster oblongifolius Nutt.

(COMPOSITE FAMILY)

Aromatic aster is an erect, highly branched perennial 6–18 in. tall arising from creeping rhizomes. The stem and leaves are covered with short hairs. The alternate leaves of the primary stems are oblong to lance-oblong and sessile, ¾–1 in. long. Short axillary stem branches with small linear leaves appear as the plant matures. The inflorescence is a panicle of head flowers ¾–1 in. across. The ray florets are violet to bluish-purple and the disks yellow. The fruit is a small silky achene.

This plant is similar to heath aster but has fewer and larger heads.

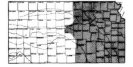

SEPTEMBER–OCTOBER

◄ **Silky Aster**

Aster sericeus Vent.

(COMPOSITE FAMILY)

Silky aster is a slender, erect perennial with smooth, wiry stems, brownish-red in color. The alternate, lanceolate to oblong leaves are silvery-silky. By flowering, the leaves of the primary stem have fallen, and small reduced leaves remain on the flowering branches that grade into squarrose phyllaries. The heads are several in a widely branched, flattopped inflorescence. The deep violet to rose-purple ray florets (15 to 25) form a head ¾–1 in. across with a yellow disk. The fruit is an achene with a brownish pappus.

The early leaves of this plant are soft and silky and provide as much beauty as the inflorescence.

49

Groundplum Milkvetch ▶

Astragalus crassicarpus Nutt. var. *crassicarpus*

(PEA FAMILY)

Groundplum milkvetch is a prostrate perennial with reddish, minutely hairy clustered stems 4–12 in. long. The alternate appressed-pilose leaves are pinnately compound with 15 to 23 leaflets ⅜–⅝ in. long. The inflorescence is a moderately dense raceme with light purple pealike flowers about ¾ in. long. The legume is a plump, succulent, reddish-green pod about ¾ in. in diameter.

The fruit of groundplum milkvetch is edible either raw or cooked and can be made into spiced pickles. Care should be taken in eating members of the genus *Astragalus* since some, called "locos," are poisonous.

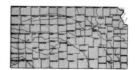

50

◄ **Wooly Loco**

Astragalus mollissimus Torr.

(PEA FAMILY)

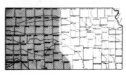

Wooly loco is a tufted, semidecumbent perennial with whitish-gray pilose stems. The alternate leaves are pinnately compound with 21 to 31 obovate to ovate leaflets which are densely silky with yellowish hairs. The inflorescence is a dense raceme 2–4 in. long with purple to violet pea flowers. The legume is a glabrous pod ½ in. long or longer.

This beautiful prairie wildflower is an unwanted guest on livestock ranches because of its highly toxic nature. One of the first green plants to appear in the spring, it can become part of cattle diets. Once they have eaten a small amount they become addicted and seek it out. It is highly unpalatable, however, and not often taken. Another problem may be poisoning of bees visiting the plant for its nectar.

JUNE–AUGUST

◄ **Purple Poppymallow**

Callirhoe involucrata (T. & G.) Gray

(MALLOW FAMILY)

Purple poppymallow is a decumbent, hirsute perennial growing from a thickened deep taproot. The leaves are orbicular to triangular and palmately divided into narrow and redivided lobes. The flower stalks have but 1 purple to wine-colored flower subtended by 3 small, narrow bracts. The flower has 5 overlapping petals forming a cup-shaped corolla with a central column of stamens loosely united by the filaments enclosing numerous styles. The fruit is of separate carpels.

The root of this plant may be eaten raw or fried in butter and produces a tasty meal. Indians have used boiled purple poppymallow roots for intestinal pains and have burned them and inhaled the smoke for colds. **51**

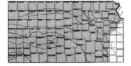

AUGUST–SEPTEMBER
Tall Thistle ▶

Cirsium altissimum (L.) Spreng.

(COMPOSITE FAMILY)

Tall thistle is an erect biennial 3–9 ft tall with a pilose stem. The alternate leaves are sessile to partly clasping, lanceolate to oblanceolate, nearly glabrous above, and densely white-tomentose below. The margins of the leaf are spiny-toothed to spiny-lobed. The rayless terminal heads are borne on leafy peduncles and have light purple disk florets subtended by a spiny involucre. The fruit is a small achene with a plumose pappus.

MAY–SEPTEMBER
◀ Yellowspine Thistle

Cirsium ochrocentrum Gray

(COMPOSITE FAMILY)

Yellowspine thistle is an erect biennial 2–4 ft tall, densely white-tomentose throughout. The alternate leaves are deeply pinnatifid into triangular-lanceolate, serrate, or entire segments with numerous long yellow spines. The upper surface of the wavy leaf is not as tomentose as the lower. The inflorescence is of terminal, rayless heads with rose-purple (rarely white) disk florets. The involucre has stout spine-tipped bracts. The fruit is a small achene with a plumose pappus.

52

◄ **Wavyleaf Thistle**

Cirsium undulatum (Nutt.) Spreng.

(COMPOSITE FAMILY)

Wavyleaf thistle is an erect biennial usually 2–3 ft tall. The stem and leaves are densely white-tomentose, particularly on the underside of the leaves. The alternate lanceolate leaves are wavy and coarsely toothed to lobed with sharp spines on the tips and along the margins. The solitary to several heads have only tubular lavender disk florets subtended by spiny involucral bracts. The fruit is a small achene with a plumose pappus.

Indians ate the stems and roots of this plant raw or cooked.

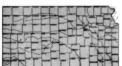

APRIL–MAY

◄ **Fremont Clematis**

Clematis fremontii Wats.

(BUTTERCUP FAMILY)

Fremont clematis is an erect perennial 6–12 in. tall with a fibrous root system. The dense leaves are opposite, broadly ovate to elliptic, with a thick, leathery texture. The leaf margin is entire (with rare teeth), and the leaf blade is sparsely villous to glabrous. The solitary apetalous flowers are borne on a recurved stalk and are composed of 4 to 5 thick lanceolate sepals. The urn-shaped calyx cup is purple on the outer surface and white within. The fruit is an achene, tipped with a persistent silken, threadlike style.

This plant has been called leatherplant because of the texture of the leaves and flower, and rattleweed because the dried plant on the prairie rattles when shaken or when the wind sweeps it across the prairie.

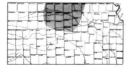

53

◀ Leavenworth Eryngo

Eryngium leavenworthii T. & G.

(PARSLEY FAMILY)

Leavenworth eryngo is an erect, glabrous perennial 1–3 ft tall. The alternate lower leaves are oblanceolate and spiny-toothed, 1–4 in. long, grading upward on the stem to palmately cleft or parted, the upper segments incised-pinnatifid and spiny. The upper leaves and bracts are purple-violet and are most striking following senescence. The umbellate heads are ovoid-ellipsoid with pinnatifid, spiny, ascending bracts. The white to blue flower is inconspicuous.

This plant resembles a thistle, but is in the carrot family. Its use in dry arrangements provides both color and curiosity.

MAY–AUGUST

◀ Largeflower Prairiegentian

Eustoma grandiflorum (Raf.) Shinners

(GENTIAN FAMILY)

Largeflower prairiegentian is a glabrous, erect annual 1–2 ft tall and branching above. The opposite, sessile leaves clasp the stem and are ovate to oblong. The inflorescence is usually a solitary flower with 5 to 6 purple to lavender-purple petals joined at the base to form a tube. The anthers are yellow and prominent, and the 2-lobed stigma is striking.

The corolla is bell-shaped and the plant is sometimes referred to as bluebell.

Rosering Gaillardia ►

Gaillardia pulchella Foug.

(COMPOSITE FAMILY)

Rosering gaillardia is an erect, branched annual 1–2 ft tall with several hirsute, grooved stems from a single base. The alternate leaves are densely hispid above and sparsely long-pubescent below. The lower leaves are oblanceolate or oblong, bluntly toothed or lobed, and sessile. The upper leaves are lanceolate, entire or wavy-margined, and sessile. The heads are solitary on long peduncles with yellow-tipped, rose-purple, 3-cleft rays. The spherical disk has dark reddish-purple florets and long bristles from the receptacle. The fruit is a densely hirsute achene.

Another common name for this plant is indianblanket.

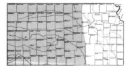

SEPTEMBER–OCTOBER
◄ Downy Gentian

Gentiana puberulenta Pringle

(GENTIAN FAMILY)

Downy gentian is an erect perennial 6–12 in. tall with a glabrous to puberulent stem. The opposite leaves are lanceolate to oblong-ovate, stiff, and with a scabrous margin. The inflorescence is crowded at the summit, forming a cluster in the upper leaf axils. The purple-blue flowers are upright and tubular, the corolla having 2-cleft plicate folds between the lobes. The seed is small, white, and winged.

The flowers of downy gentian close toward evening or on cloudy days. The gentian is named in honor of Gentius, King of Illyrica from 180 to 167 B.C., who was thought to be the first to discover its medicinal value. However, the Egyptians apparently used it thousands of years earlier. Its principal use has been in the treatment of bites and stings.

55

◄ **Tall Gayfeather**

Liatris aspera Michx.

(COMPOSITE FAMILY)

Tall gayfeather is an erect perennial 2–4 ft tall, glabrous throughout, arising from a well-developed corm. The alternate leaves are numerous, rough, and linear. The inflorescence is a spike of rayless purple to lavender heads. The involucral bracts are inrolled at the edges and have an attractive buttonlike appearance. The achene has a barbellate pappus.

If the plant is dried just prior to opening of the flowers, it makes an attractive addition to dried arrangements.

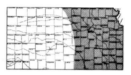

AUGUST–OCTOBER

Dotted Gayfeather ►

Liatris punctata Hook.

(COMPOSITE FAMILY)

Dotted gayfeather is an erect perennial 1–2 ft tall arising from a well-developed corm, a thickened caudex, or a stout rhizome. The numerous alternate leaves are linear, glabrous, and punctate. The margin of the leaf is sometimes coarsely ciliate. The heads are crowded into a partially leafy spike. The rays are absent and the disk florets are rose-purple. The achene has plumose bristles.

The root of this species may be cooked and eaten. The boiled root has been used by Indians for swellings and for intestinal pains. The Indians called this plant crow-root because ravens and crows were seen eating the root in autumn.

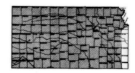

◄ Thickspike Gayfeather

Liatris pycnostachya Michx.

(COMPOSITE FAMILY)

Thickspike gayfeather is an erect perennial 2–5 ft tall, more or less hirsute throughout, arising from a woody corm. The numerous alternate leaves are linear, punctate, and entire. The cylindric inflorescence is spikelike, with crowded sessile heads. The discoid head has rose-purple florets and is subtended by squarrose involucral bracts. The fruit is an angled achene with a barbellate pappus.

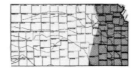

JUNE–AUGUST

◄ Tansyleaf Aster

Machaeranthera tanacetifolia (H.B.K.) Nees.

(COMPOSITE FAMILY)

Tansyleaf aster is an erect, highly branched annual 12–18 in. tall. The stem and leaves are glandular-pubescent throughout. The alternate leaves are generally pinnatifid, the lower ones sometimes twice-divided. The inflorescence is composed of heads terminating the branches. The heads have red-violet to violet-purple rays and yellow disk florets. The fruit is a pubescent achene.

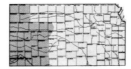

57

JUNE–AUGUST
Mintleaf Beebalm
Monarda fistulosa L. var. *fistulosa*

(MINT FAMILY)

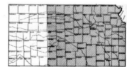

Mintleaf beebalm is an erect, aromatic perennial 2–4 ft tall arising from a branched rhizome. The often-branched stem is square and usually pubescent. The opposite leaves are commonly deltoid-lanceolate, pubescent, and more or less serrate. Both leaves and flowers are dotted with glands which secrete volatile, aromatic oils. The inflorescence is a hemispheric head with tubular pale lavender to rose-purple flowers with bilabiate corollas mixed with leafy bracts. The upper lip of the corolla is densely villous at the summit. The fruit is composed of 4 nutlets.

The aroma from dried leaves of this plant can be used to freshen closets, trunks, and other areas. A tea from the dried leaves has a delightful aroma and a pleasing taste. Oil from this plant has also been used as a fixative in perfumes. Thymol, an antiseptic drug, can be extracted from the plant. Dried leaves are said to be good for nausea and for vomiting in bilious fevers. The Choctaw Indians gave it as a cathartic, for colds, and to promote perspiration.

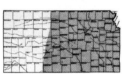

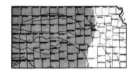

MAY–JUNE
Violet Woodsorrel Oxalis

Oxalis violacea L.

(WOODSORREL FAMILY)

Violet woodsorrel oxalis is an erect perennial 4–12 in. tall arising from a scaly, bulbous base. The glabrous leaves are all basal, palmately trifoliolate, and succulent. The leaflets are obovate to obcordate, notched at the tip, gray-green to bluish-green above, and reddish-purple below. Flowers are borne in umbelliform clusters with 5-petaled lavender-pink to rose-violet corollas. The capsule is ovoid or globose.

The edible properties of this plant are similar to those of common yellow oxalis. Leaves of all members of this genus fold downward at dusk or in cloudy weather and open during daylight hours, a phenomenon called "sleep movement." American Indians put ground bulbs of this plant in their horses' feed to make them faster. The salts of oxalic acid of this plant can be used to remove ink spots. The capsules at maturity invert rapidly, flinging the seeds away from the plant.

MAY–JULY
Lambert Crazyweed

Oxytropis lambertii Pursh

(PEA FAMILY)

Lambert crazyweed is a tufted perennial 6–12 in. tall, appearing stemless. The alternate leaves are pinnately compound, with 9 to 21 linear to narrowly oblong leaflets, and more or less silky with appressed hairs. The leaflets are acutely tipped and ascending. The inflorescence is an axillary spike borne on long peduncles of purple to bluish-purple (sometimes light yellow) pea flowers. The fruit is a cylindric glabrous pod with a distinct beak.

Though extremely unpalatable, lambert crazyweed is sometimes eaten by livestock and causes disorientation, loss of muscle control, and sometimes death. Poisoning is most common early in the growing season on overgrazed range. This plant is commonly mistaken for wooly loco, but may be differentiated by the pointed leaf tips and keel of lambert crazyweed as opposed to a rounded tip and keel of wooly loco. Often patches of this plant will have both yellow- and purple-flowered plants.

59

Cobaea Penstemon ▶

Penstemon cobaea Nutt.

(SNAPDRAGON FAMILY)

Cobaea penstemon is an erect perennial 1–2 ft tall, finely pubescent throughout. The opposite leaves are sessile above and short-petioled below, ovate-elliptic or obovate, and sharply toothed. The inflorescence is racemelike, arranged in few-flowered clusters in leaf axils with bracts interspersed. The light purple to purple corolla is tubular, trumpet-shaped, with 5 rounded lobes, and with dark purple striping within. As with other penstemons, it has a bearded staminode. The fruit is an ovoid capsule.

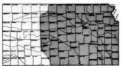

◀ Shell-leaf Penstemon

Penstemon grandiflorus Nutt.

(SNAPDRAGON FAMILY)

Shell-leaf penstemon is an erect perennial 1–3 ft tall with glabrous stems and leaves. The opposite leaves are obovate-oblong, fleshy, bluish-green, and somewhat clasping at the base. The leaf margin is entire. The inflorescence is racemelike with tubular, bell-shaped, pale purple flowers. The corolla has 5 lobes and a bearded staminode. The fruit is an obovoid capsule.

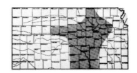

60

◄ Purple Prairieclover

Petalostemon purpureum (Vent.) Rydb.

(PEA FAMILY)

Purple prairieclover is a slender, erect perennial 1–2 ft tall growing from a short, vertical rootstock. The alternate, pinnately compound leaves have 3 to 7 leaflets, usually 5. The narrowly linear leaflets are glabrous to pilose and glandular-punctate beneath. The inflorescence is a compressed cylindric spike of small purple to red-purple flowers. The flowers are not pealike, only 1 petal being well developed. The other apparent petals are actually staminodes. The fruit is a small legume, remaining enclosed in the densely villous calyx.

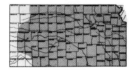

Bruised leaves of this plant steeped in water were applied to fresh wounds by Indians. The Comanche chewed the roots and made a tea from the leaves.

MAY–AUGUST
◄ Resinous Skullcap

Scutellaria resinosa Torr.

(MINT FAMILY)

Resinous skullcap is an erect, clustered perennial 6–12 in. tall arising from a single crown. The opposite leaves are ovate to elliptic and finely pubescent. The inflorescence is of axillary blue to purple flowers. The corolla is 2-lipped, the upper lip usually concave, the lower flat, 4-lobed, and with 2 white bars near the center. The fruit is composed of 4 nutlets.

◄ **Fineleaf Tomanthera**

Tomanthera densiflora Benth.

(SNAPDRAGON FAMILY)

Fineleaf tomanthera is an erect, highly branched annual 1–2 ft tall. Stems and leaves are bristly throughout. The opposite leaves are pinnately parted into narrow, linear segments. The tubular purple to violet flowers are borne in the upper leaf axils and are distinctly 2-lipped. The fruit is a small oval capsule.

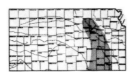

JUNE–AUGUST
◄ **Wooly Verbena**

Verbena stricta Vent.

(VERVAIN FAMILY)

Wooly verbena is an erect perennial 1–3 ft tall, densely hirsute throughout. The opposite leaves are ovate to elliptic, sessile, and sharply serrate to doubly serrate. The inflorescence is a dense spike of blue to purple (rarely white) flowers subtended by bracts. The tubular corolla consists of 4 united petals, flared at the top and 4-lobed. The fruit is composed of 4 ellipsoid nutlets.

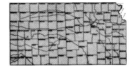

Baldwin Ironweed ▶

Vernonia baldwini Torr. var. *interior* (Small) Schub.

(COMPOSITE FAMILY)

Baldwin ironweed is an erect perennial 2–4 ft tall with thinly pubescent to tomentose stems. The alternate leaves are ovate-lanceolate to ovate, sharply serrate, pubescent above, and tomentose beneath. The inflorescence is usually a flattopped panicle of rose-purple to lavender heads of disk florets only. The seed is a small, resinous, pubescent achene with a fluffy brown pappus.

MAY–JULY

◀ Stiffleaf Vetch

Vicia americana Muhl. var. *minor* Hook.

(PEA FAMILY)

Stiffleaf vetch is a weak-stemmed, semidecumbent perennial 6–12 in. tall, essentially glabrous. The pinnately compound, alternate leaves have 8 to 14 leaflets and are tipped with a terminal, often-branched tendril. The inflorescence is a few-flowered raceme of large purple to purplish pea flowers. The legume is a slender glabrous pod with a persistent calyx.

◄ **Prairie Violet**

Viola pedatifida G. Don

(VIOLET FAMILY)

Prairie violet is a low, erect perennial 4–10 in. tall with the crown developing on an erect rhizome. The leaves and flower stalks arise directly from that crown. The leaves are 3-parted, each division 3-cleft again, forming linear lobes. The flowers are borne on a long recurved peduncle. The zygomorphic corolla has 5 violet to blue petals—2 upper, 2 lateral, and a lower petal with a spur—and is bearded at the throat. The fruit is a yellowish, prism-shaped, 3-parted capsule.

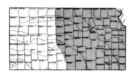

K E Y / *Yellow Flowers*

1a. Flowers with free petals (polypetalous)
  2a. Regular corolla (radial symmetry)
    3a. Alternate leaves
      4a. Simple leaves
        5a. Margin entire
          6a. Petals 4, 141, 163, 168, 169
          6b. Petals 5, 164, 193
        5b. Margin not entire
          6a. Toothed, 129, 130, 141
          6b. Pinnatifid, 167
          6c. Cleft or parted, 166
      4b. Palmately compound, 172
    3b. Opposite leaves, 162
    3c. Spirally arranged leaves, 170
  2b. Irregular corolla (bilateral symmetry)
    3a. Alternate leaves
      4a. Simple leaves, 6
      4b. Compound leaves
        5a. Pinnately compound, 114, 131, 133, 139
        5b. Palmately compound, 128
    3b. Opposite leaves, 66

1b. Flowers with fused petals (sympetalous)
  2a. Regular corolla (radial symmetry)
    3a. Alternate leaves
      4a. Margin entire
        5a. Flowers in a head
          6a. Heads with long rays (>½ in.), 142, 153, 161, 175, 176
          6b. Heads with short rays (<½ in.)
            7a. Leaves with hairs, 160, 185, 190
            7b. Leaves without hairs, 145, 146, 189
        5b. Flowers not in a head, 165
      4b. Margin not entire
        5a. Toothed
          6a. Flowers in a head
            7a. Heads with yellow disk
              8a. Heads with short rays (<1 in.)
                9a. Inflorescence not clustered, 143, 147, 149
                9b. Inflorescence clustered, 183, 184, 186, 187
              8b. Heads with long rays (>1 in.), 152, 153, 154
            7b. Heads with disk not yellow, 150, 155, 176, 177
          6b. Flowers not in a head, 73, 137
        5b. Pinnatifid
          6a. Flowers in a head, 140, 148, 173, 174, 180
          6b. Flowers not in a head, 182
        5c. Lobed, 174, 177, 178
    3b. Opposite leaves
      4a. Simple leaves
        5a. Pinnatifid, 136, 188
        5b. Toothed, 156, 157, 159, 179, 181
      4b. Pinnately compound leaves, 135
  2b. Irregular corolla (bilateral symmetry), 73, 134, 190

65

◀ **Plains Wildindigo**

Baptisia leucophaea Nutt.

(PEA FAMILY)

Plains wildindigo is a bushy perennial with spreading, branched stems, hairy throughout. The leaves are palmately trifoliolate, with oblanceolate leaflets and 2 large leaflike stipules giving the appearance of 5 leaflets. The inflorescence consists of drooping, dense racemes of large yellow pea flowers. The legumes are ovoid, 1–2½ in. long, terminating in a beak.

A decoction of the leaves of this plant was used by Indians as a stimulant and for application to cuts and wounds. An infusion made from the roots was also used as a remedy for typhoid and scarlet fever.

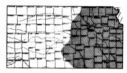

JUNE–SEPTEMBER

◀ **Lavenderleaf Eveningprimrose**

Calylophus hartwegii (Benth.) Raven ssp. *lavandulifolius* (T. & G.) Towner & Raven

(EVENINGPRIMROSE FAMILY)

Lavenderleaf eveningprimrose is a tufted perennial 6–12 in. tall with ascending canescent branches arising from a woody base. The alternate leaves are numerous, crowded, linear-oblong to lanceolate, sharply dentate, and canescent. The flowers are solitary in the upper leaf axils and have 4 yellow, crinkled petals. The stigma is discoid rather than lobed or toothed as are many other species of *Oenothera*. The fruit is a cylindric capsule, more or less curved.

This plant was formerly in the genus *Oenothera*.

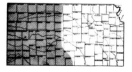

Serrateleaf Eveningprimrose ▶

MAY–JULY

Calylophus serrulatus (Nutt.) Raven

(EVENINGPRIMROSE FAMILY)

Serrateleaf eveningprimrose is an erect perennial 6–18 in. tall with simple or branched stems, woody at the base, and glabrate to silvery-canescent. The alternate leaves are linear-oblong to lanceolate, sharply dentate, and glabrous to canescent. The flowers are sessile in the upper leaf axils and have 4 yellow petals. The flower is borne atop a hypanthium which extends above the ovary. The fruit is a linear-cylindric capsule with a persistent calyx.

This plant was formerly in the genus *Oenothera*.

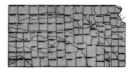

JULY–SEPTEMBER

◀ Showy Partridgepea

Cassia fasciculata Michx.

(PEA FAMILY)

Showy partridgepea is an erect, highly branched annual 1–4 ft tall. The 2-ranked leaves are alternate and evenly pinnately compound with 14–26 oblong, inequilateral leaflets. The leaflets are sparsely hairy on the margins and distinctly veined. The compound leaf has a reddish-brown gland near the base. The yellow flowers are clustered in the leaf axils, 2 to 6 or more. The flower has 5 free petals and 6 to 7 large, drooping red-violet anthers. The legume is highly flattened and linear, 2–4 in. long.

The leaves of this plant are touch-sensitive and the leaflets fold together when handled. Seeds of showy partridgepea are reputed to be excellent quail food. This plant is usually found only in disturbed sites, primarily in roadside ditches.

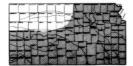

67

YELLOW FLOWERS

◄ Wild Senna

Cassia marilandica L.

(PEA FAMILY)

Wild senna is an erect perennial 3–6 ft tall, glabrous throughout, with creeping rhizomes. The alternate leaves are evenly pinnately compound with 4 to 8 pairs of oblong or elliptic leaflets. The petiole has a prominent gland near its base. The inflorescence is composed of several axillary and terminal racemes. The flowers have 5 free yellow petals with 1 petal being slightly larger than the others. The 10 dark red stamens vary in shape and attachment. The fruit is a flat, thin, partitioned legume.

The leaves and pods of this plant are used as a laxative.

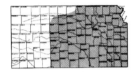

MAY–JULY

◄ Downy Paintbrush

Castilleja sessiliflora Pursh

(SNAPDRAGON FAMILY)

Downy paintbrush is a leafy, pubescent perennial ½–1½ ft tall, usually with several stems growing from a single base. The alternate upper leaves are cleft to below the middle into 3 to 5 divergent lobes. The inflorescence is a dense spike 1–2 in. long of tubular yellowish flowers with a long tubular green calyx deeply 2-cleft. Flowers prior to opening are tinged pink. The upper lip of the corolla is about twice as long as the lower one. The fruit is a many-seeded capsule. Members of this genus are root parasites, usually on members of the aster family.

◄ **Bigflower Coreopsis**

Coreopsis grandiflora Hogg

(COMPOSITE FAMILY)

Bigflower coreopsis is an erect or ascending, highly branched, glabrous perennial 1–3 ft tall with slender stems arising from a short rhizome. The opposite leaves are pinnately compound or deeply lobed, the divisions linear or lanceolate. The basal and lower leaves are petioled, the upper leaves sessile or nearly so. The inflorescence is of terminal heads with yellow ray florets and yellowish-brown disk florets. The fruit is an orbicular winged achene.

MAY–SEPTEMBER
◄ **Plains Coreopsis**

Coreopsis tinctora Nutt.

(COMPOSITE FAMILY)

Plains coreopsis is an erect to ascending, glabrous annual 1–3 ft tall with several slender, branched stems. The opposite leaves are once- or twice-pinnately divided into narrow linear segments, the upper less divided. The inflorescence is composed of solitary heads on peduncles arising from the upper leaf axils. The heads have yellow ray florets with a brown to reddish-brown band at the base and are toothed at the apex. The disk is yellowish-brown and produces a wingless linear achene.

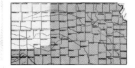

69

Buffalogourd ►

Cucurbita foetidissima H. B. K.

(GOURD FAMILY)

Buffalogourd is a prostrate, viny perennial from a thick rootstock. The stems are coarse and rough, often several yards long, with tendrils. The grayish-green leaves are triangular-ovate, 4–6 in. long, and with a finely toothed margin and rough on both sides. The flowers are solitary in the leaf axils with a yellow, tubular, 5-lobed corolla. The plants are monoecious, with male and female flowers on the same plant. The male flowers are more numerous than the female. The fruit is fleshy (pepo) and nearly globose, about the size of a tennis ball, with yellow and green stripes.

The fruit pulp and root of buffalogourd have enough saponin to make them a soap substitute. The fruit can be eaten, but is decidedly bitter. Several medicinal qualities have been attributed to the roots of this plant. Among them are cures for rheumatism, constipation, and sores and ulcers. The Navajo used dried gourds for rattles in ceremonials.

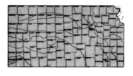

JULY–AUGUST
◄ Silktop Dalea

Dalea aurea Nutt.

(PEA FAMILY)

Silktop dalea is a perennial 1–2 ft tall with a strong taproot and a scant-leaved upright stem. The plant is clad throughout with short, appressed, silky hairs, making it grayish- to whitish-green in appearance. The alternate leaves are pinnately compound with 5 to 9 obovate leaflets. The inflorescence is a dense terminal spike of yellow pea flowers. The legume is usually 1-seeded, remaining enclosed in a persistent calyx.

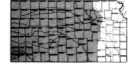

◄ **Engelmanndaisy**

Engelmannia pinnatifida T. & G.

(COMPOSITE FAMILY)

Engelmanndaisy is an erect to spreading perennial 1–3 ft tall arising from a branching crown with a thick taproot. The bristly stems have alternate, pinnatifid, simple leaves with progressively shorter petioles upward on the stem. The inflorescence is simple to flattopped, composed of yellow heads. The 8 to 10 ray florets and the disk florets are bright yellow. The fruit is a ciliate achene with a pappus resembling a low-cleft crown.

MAY–JUNE

Plains Erysimum ►

(Western Wallflower)

Erysimum asperum (Nutt.) DC.

(MUSTARD FAMILY)

Plains erysimum is a stiff, erect perennial 6–18 in. tall, simple or branched above. The alternate leaves are linear to oblanceolate, entire or with a few teeth, and thinly to densely pubescent. The inflorescence forms a hemispheric raceme of 4-petaled yellow to orange flowers. The fruit is thin, 4-angled, and 3–5 in. long, and sticking straight out to slightly upwards from the stem.

71

◄ **Prairie Gaillardia**

Gaillardia fastigiata Greene

(COMPOSITE FAMILY)

Prairie gaillardia is an erect, branched biennial 1–2 ft tall with dense, short pubescence. The alternate basal leaves are spatulate, with wavy margins. The upper leaves are lance-linear, alternate, and wavy-margined. The stems and leaves have short, rough hairs. Heads terminate the branches and have 3-cleft yellow rays and a dark purple hemispheric disk with long bristles growing from the receptacle. The fruit is an achene with a series of awn-tipped scales.

JULY–OCTOBER
◄ **Curlycup Gumweed**

Grindelia squarrosa (Pursh) Dun. var. *squarrosa*

(COMPOSITE FAMILY)

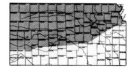

Curlycup gumweed is a highly branched, erect biennial or perennial 2–4 ft tall, glabrous throughout. The alternate leaves are simple, ovate to ovate-spatulate, and with a serrate margin, the bases partly clasping the stem. Leaves are abundantly resinous-punctate. The branched upper stems terminate in ½–1 in. diameter yellow heads. The involucral bracts are linear-lanceolate, mostly recurved, giving the curlycup appearance, and are very resinous. The ray and head florets are bright yellow. The fruit is an achene with 2 to 8 awned pappi.

The resinous character of the plant gives rise to the name gumweed. The plant is usually found in disturbed areas in the prairie. Honey from bees collecting gumweed nectar is poor flavored and granular. The leaves, dried or green, make an excellent tea. The list of medicinal uses of the leaves and head is long; included are treatments for indigestion, throat and lung troubles, itching, colic, and poison-oak irritation.

◄ Broomweed

Gutierrezia dracunculoides (DC.) Blake

(COMPOSITE FAMILY)

Broomweed is a bushy-branched, erect annual 1–2 ft tall, glabrous throughout. The alternate sessile leaves are linear and ½–2 in. long. The heads are numerous and solitary at the ends of slender branches. The ray florets (6 to 10) have yellow ligulate petals and the yellow disk florets (10 to 20) are borne on a hemispheric involucre. The fruit is an achene with a crownlike pappus.

This annual plant is usually associated with open stands of vegetation as occur with overgrazing or disturbance.

◄ Broom Snakeweed

Gutierrezia sarothrae (Pursh) Britt. & Rusby

(COMPOSITE FAMILY)

Broom snakeweed is a half shrub perennial 1–2 ft tall, woody at the base of the stems, and herbaceous and highly branched above. The glabrous leaves are alternate, linear, and 1–2 in. long. The heads are crowded in small clusters of 2 to 5 heads at the ends of the branches. The ray florets are short, yellow, and 6 to 10 in number. The disk florets are yellow and 3 to 4 in number. The fruit is an achene with 5 to 9 chaffy scales or bristles.

Indians used the stems of this plant tied together for brooms. They also used a decoction from the leaves to treat stomachache, snakebite, and rheumatism.

73

◄ Wax Goldenweed

Haplopappus ciliatus (Nutt.) DC.

(COMPOSITE FAMILY)

___

Wax goldenweed is an erect, glabrous annual or biennial 2–5 ft tall, the stem commonly simple to near the top. The alternate leaves are sessile, clasping, oval or obovate, and sharply toothed with bristle-pointed teeth. The heads are few and clustered at the ends of the branches with yellow ray and disk florets. The fruit is a glabrous, several-nerved achene with a pappus of a few deciduous, unequal bristles.

MAY–AUGUST

◄ Ironplant

Haplopappus spinulosus (Pursh) DC.

(COMPOSITE FAMILY)

___

Ironplant is an erect perennial arising from a woody base with a thick woody taproot. The alternate, simple leaves are sessile and pinnatifid, the lobes bristle-tipped. The several heads have yellow ray and disk florets. The fruit is a hairy achene with the pappus a series of 1 to 3 persistent capillary bristles.

The name ironplant derives from the dried specimen having an extremely hard, woody base. In Mexico this plant is sold in markets by the name "yerba de la vivora" as a blood purifier.

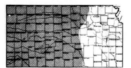

74

◄ Slender Goldenweed

Haplopappus validus (Rydb.) Cory

(COMPOSITE FAMILY)

Slender goldenweed is an erect, slender annual 1–2 ft tall, highly branched above the middle. The stems vary from subglabrous to hairy and are often glandular. The alternate leaves are oblanceolate to linear-lanceolate, having a few spiny teeth and a few long hairs near the base. The small heads are numerous in a diffuse panicle with yellow ray and disk florets. The fruit is a canescent achene with a persistent plumose pappus.

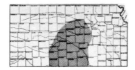

JULY–SEPTEMBER

Common Sunflower

Helianthus annuus L.

(COMPOSITE FAMILY)

Common sunflower is a robust, erect annual 3–12 ft tall. The stout stem is scabrous-hispid, with alternate, long-petioled leaves, cordate-ovate to elliptic-oval in shape. The leaf blade is rough on both surfaces with a dentate margin. The heads are solitary, with yellow ray florets 1–3 in. long. The disk is brown and up to 2 in. across. The fruit is a flattened achene with a pappus of 2 awns.

No book on Kansas prairie wildflowers would be complete without the state flower. Though commonly found in waste or disturbed areas, it is sometimes found in prairies. While still growing, sunflowers, as the name indicates, do indeed follow the sun with the leaves and flowers. Sunflower oil is commonly extracted for use in cooking, paints, soaps, and even hair oil. The seed can be eaten raw or parched or ground and used in bread and cakes. Purple and black dyes have been made from the seeds and yellow dyes from the flowers. The roasted shells have been used as a coffee substitute. Even the pith of the plant has been used in life preservers. Breeding selections of this species are common cultivated crops in many areas of the world today.

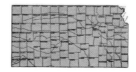

75

◄ Sawtooth Sunflower

Helianthus grosseserratus Martens

(COMPOSITE FAMILY)

Sawtooth sunflower is an erect perennial 5–9 ft tall with glabrous stems arising from an elongate rhizome; the plants form colonies. The alternate leaves are lanceolate, petiolate, and coarsely toothed. The leaf blades are harshly scabrous above and densely pubescent beneath. The heads are borne on the upper branches and peduncles and have yellow ray and disk florets. The fruit is a flattened achene.

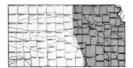

AUGUST–OCTOBER

◄ Maximilian Sunflower

Helianthus maximiliani Schrad.

(COMPOSITE FAMILY)

Maximilian sunflower is an erect perennial of several stems 3–6 ft tall arising from short rhizomes and is rough-pubescent throughout. The simple alternate leaves are sessile or very short petioled and are lanceolate to linear-lanceolate in shape. The blade of the leaf is conduplicate or trough-shaped, with an entire or scarcely toothed margin. The numerous terminal heads have yellow disks and 15 to 30 yellow rays. The fruit is a flattened achene, oblong-obovate and glabrous.

Indians ate the tuberous root of this plant raw or cooked.

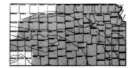

◄ **Ashy Sunflower**

Helianthus mollis Lam.

(COMPOSITE FAMILY)

Ashy sunflower is an erect perennial 2–4 ft tall growing from well-developed rhizomes and with densely villous stems. The opposite leaves are sessile, clasping the stem, with a subcordate base, and ovate to ovate-lanceolate. The leaf blade is densely whitish-hairy on both surfaces and the margin entire to slightly toothed. Heads are solitary or few, terminal, and with yellow ray and disk florets. The fruit is a flattened achene. The entire plant has a whitish-gray appearance.

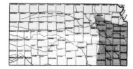

JULY–SEPTEMBER
Prairie Sunflower ►

Helianthus petiolaris Nutt.

(COMPOSITE FAMILY)

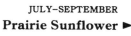

Prairie sunflower is an erect, branched annual 2–6 ft tall with villous stems toward the summit. The alternate leaves are narrowly oblong-lanceolate to deltoid-ovate, petiolate, strigose-pilose, and with entire or undulate-dentate margins. The heads are several to numerous, terminating the branches, with yellow rays and a purplish-brown disk. The fruit is a compressed achene.

This plant is a diminutive of common sunflower and grows almost exclusively on sand.

77

◄ **Stiff Sunflower**

Helianthus rigidus (Cass.) Desf. spp. *subrhomboideus* (Rydb.) Heiser

(COMPOSITE FAMILY)

Stiff sunflower is an erect perennial 2–5 ft tall with simple, scabrous stems and well-developed, stout, creeping rhizomes. The opposite leaves are sparse on the stem, broadly lanceolate to narrowly ovate, and scabrous. The leaf margin is serrate and the leaf folds, more or less, forming a trough-like shape. The heads are usually solitary, but may be several. The disk is purple to purplish-brown with 15 to 20 yellow rays. The achene is oblong-obovate with 2 long awns.

The leathery, stiff leaves give rise to the name stiff sunflower.

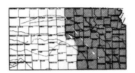

JULY–SEPTEMBER

◄ **Jerusalemartichoke**

Helianthus tuberosus L.

(COMPOSITE FAMILY)

Jerusalemartichoke is an erect perennial with well-developed tuberous rhizomes. The stems are stout, more or less pubescent, and branching above. The leaves are usually opposite, the uppermost sometimes alternate. Leaf blades are ovate-lanceolate to oblong-lanceolate with a rough upper surface and smooth below. Heads are numerous in a panicle with a yellow disk and 10 to 20 yellow rays. The fruit is a flattened achene.

The tubers of Jerusalemartichoke are formed late in the growing season—late October and early November. The name Jerusalem is not of Middle East origin, but comes from the word "girasole" which is Italian for sunflower. The tuber may be eaten raw or cooked and has been dried and pickled as a relish. It also yields insulin and sugars. One author speculates the tuber may become an important source for alcohol and synthetic rubber.

JUNE–AUGUST

Rough Heliopsis

Heliopsis helianthoides (L.) Sweet var. *scabra* (Dun.) Fern.

(COMPOSITE FAMILY)

Rough heliopsis is an erect, short-lived perennial 2–6 ft tall arising from a short rhizome with glabrous to scabrous stems. The opposite leaves are petiolate, ovate to lance-ovate, sharply serrate, and rough on both surfaces. Heads are solitary or several, terminating the branches, and have yellow ray and disk florets. The fruit is a quadrangular glabrous achene without a pappus.

79

◀ **Longbeard Hawkweed**

Hieracium longipilum Torr.

(COMPOSITE FAMILY)

Longbeard hawkweed is an upright perennial 2–5 ft tall represented most of the year by a leafy basal rosette. The plant is long-pilose throughout and has milky juice. The alternate leaves are oblanceolate or elliptic, mostly basal, and reduced above. The inflorescence is elongate, having several rayless heads with 40 to 90 yellow ligulate florets. The achene has a tawny, hoary pappus.

This plant has many reputed medicinal properties; among them are cures for indigestion, snakebite, toothache, and warts. The juice may be coagulated and used as a chewing gum. Old World inhabitants believed that hawks ate the sap to improve eyesight.

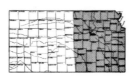

MAY–JULY

◀ **Stemless Hymenoxys**

Hymenoxys acaulis (Pursh) Parker

(COMPOSITE FAMILY)

Stemless hymenoxys is a stemless perennial 6–10 in. tall arising from a taproot and branching caudex. The leaves are all basal and tufted, linear to oblanceolate, and densely villous. The heads are borne on a naked flowering stem arising from the ground (scape) and have yellow ray and disk florets. The fruit is a small, 5-angled, hairy achene.

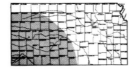

Common St. Johnswort ▶

Hypericum perforatum L.

(ST. JOHNSWORT FAMILY)

Common St. Johnswort is a highly branched, erect perennial 1–2 ft tall. The glabrous, opposite leaves are sessile, linear-oblong, and punctate throughout. The flower has 5 yellow petals, black-dotted on the margin. Numerous yellow stamens highlight the flower. The fruit is a globose capsule with small blackish seeds.

The leaves and flowers of this plant contain a photodynamic poison, hypericin, which when ingested is translocated to lightly pigmented areas of the animal and reacts with light to produce an irritation. Often slow-healing sores develop. Common St. Johnswort is reported to be of medicinal value in treating hysteria, somnambulism, and wounds.

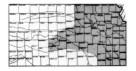

MAY–JUNE

◀ Ovalleaf Bladderpod

Lesquerella ovalifolia Rydb. spp. *ovalifolia*

(MUSTARD FAMILY)

Ovalleaf bladderpod is an erect perennial with tufted stems 4–8 in. tall. The alternate basal leaves are obovate to ovate, tapering into a long petiole. The sessile upper leaves are linear to linear-oblanceolate. The leaves are covered with a stellate whitish pubescence. The inflorescence is a short raceme of flowers with 4 yellow petals. The globose pod is tipped and borne on a short stipe and a slender, ascending pedicel.

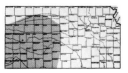

81

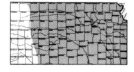

◄ Grooved Flax

Linum sulcatum Ridd.

(FLAX FAMILY)

Grooved flax is an erect annual 1–2 ft tall with a grooved stem. The alternate leaves are narrowly linear with a pair of minute dark glands at the base. The inflorescence is a panicle with yellow flowers borne at the ends of the branches. The flowers have 5 petals which usually fall on the same day the flower opens. The sepals do not fall as they do in most other *Linum* species. The fruit is an ovoid capsule.

These flowers are not good cut flowers, since the slightest agitation will cause the petals to fall.

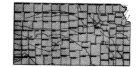

APRIL–JUNE

◄ Narrowleaf Gromwell

Lithospermum incisum Lehm.

(BORAGE FAMILY)

Narrowleaf gromwell is an erect, bristly perennial 6–18 in. tall with appressed pubescence. The alternate, simple leaves are linear to narrowly linear-lanceolate and are densely bristly. The inflorescence is a leafy raceme of yellow tubular flowers with 5 petals. The salverform corolla has 5 rounded lobes crinkled on the lacerate edges. The corolla falls off when the flower is handled. The fruit is a hard, shiny, white nutlet.

The red root of this species may be eaten cooked or used to make a dye.

APRIL–JUNE

◀ Carrotleaf Lomatium

Lomatium foeniculaceum (Nutt.) Coult. & Rose var. *daucifolium* (T. & G.) Crong.

(PARSLEY FAMILY)

Carrotleaf lomatium is a prostrate aromatic perennial 4–10 in. tall. The alternate, mostly basal leaves are divided to the base into 3 divisions, each of them 3-pinnate. The petiole of the leaf is strongly sheathing. The inflorescence is a compound umbel of 5-petaled yellow flowers. The fruit is oval with broadly winged lateral ribs.

The aroma of this plant reminds one of celery. The roots are edible raw or cooked. The young stems may also be eaten. The dried root has been ground into flour and biscuitlike cakes baked from it. The seeds may be eaten raw or dried and ground into flour.

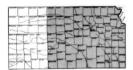

JULY–SEPTEMBER

◀ Tenpetal Mentzelia

Mentzelia decapetala (Pursh) Urban & Gilg.

(LOASA FAMILY)

Tenpetal mentzelia is an erect biennial or short-lived perennial 3–5 ft tall. The plant is armed throughout with stiff, barbed hairs. The alternate leaves are sessile, narrowly lanceolate or oblong, and sharply pinnatifid with a wavy margin. The inflorescence is terminal at the ends of the branches with 10-petaled creamy-yellow flowers which may be 2–4 in. across. The flowers remain closed during the hot part of the day. The central stamen mass is yellow and adds to the beauty of this flower.

The fruit of this plant may be parched and ground to produce a nutritious meal.

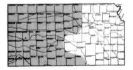

83

◄ Fremont Eveningprimrose

Oenothera fremontii Wats.

(EVENINGPRIMROSE FAMILY)

Fremont eveningprimrose is a tufted, erect perennial 2–6 in. tall arising from an elongated crown. The stems and leaves are silvery-canescent. The alternate leaves are oblong and entire. The large flowers are borne singly in the upper leaf axils and have 4 yellow petals and a long hypanthium extending well above the ovary. The fruit is a broad-winged oval to oblong capsule.

◄ Missouri Eveningprimrose

Oenothera macrocarpa Nutt. var. *macrocarpa*

(EVENINGPRIMROSE FAMILY)

Missouri eveningprimrose is a decumbent to ascending perennial 6–18 in. tall with silvery-canescent stems. The alternate leaves are linear-oblanceolate, leathery in texture, and finely silvery-pubescent. The flowers are axillary, with 4 sepals united to form a long tube (hypanthium) and 4 large, free, yellow petals. The stigma is large and 4-lobed. The fruit is an orbicular capsule 1½–3 in. long and 1½–2 in. wide with 4 broad wings.

This plant is usually associated with disturbed areas in the prairie. The flowers close during the daytime, opening toward evening.

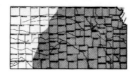

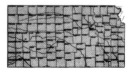

MAY–JUNE

◄ **Common Pricklypear**

Opuntia macrorhiza Engelm.

(CACTUS FAMILY)

Common pricklypear is a prostrate or spreading perennial 6–18 in. tall with spiny, fleshy stems composed of pad-like internodes separated by articulations. The leaves are scalelike on the young internodes, mostly deciduous, and spirally arranged. The flowers are solitary, with numerous rows of overlapping yellow petals, with the sepals petallike. The stamens are numerous and showy. The fruit is obovoid, pulpy, and green to dull purple.

The fruits of this plant can be peeled and the pulp eaten raw or cooked. Syrup can be made by boiling the fruit and straining off the juice. During a drouth, the spines have been singed from the pads which can then be fed to livestock as an emergency feed. Indeed, young plants with few spines are readily eaten by livestock in pasture situations. Medicinally, the plant has been used as a poultice for wounds and bruises. The fleshy pads may be a source of water in emergency situations.

85

◀ **Common Yellow Oxalis**

Oxalis stricta L.

(WOODSORREL FAMILY)

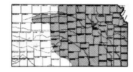

Common yellow oxalis is an erect (sometimes prostrate) perennial 4–12 in. tall with a slender, succulent stem. The alternate leaves are palmately trifoliolate with obovate to obcordate leaflets, entire or notched at the apex. The leaves and petioles are more or less pubescent, with ascendng or incurved hairs. The inflorescence is an umbel with rarely more than 3 flowers per umbel, sometimes solitary. The 5 petals are yellow, sometimes with red dots at the base. The fruit is a narrow, densely to thinly gray-pubescent capsule, erect or ascending from a deflexed pedicel.

The leaves and stems of this plant may be eaten raw and have a strongly acid taste. The acid taste comes from oxalic acid, which can cause poisoning if too much is eaten. A quantity of this plant may be allowed to ferment and makes a tasty dessert.

MAY–JULY
◀ **Upright Prairieconeflower**

Ratibida columnifera (Nutt.) Woot. & Standl.

(COMPOSITE FAMILY)

Upright prairieconeflower is an erect perennial 1–2½ ft tall with minutely pubescent stems. The alternate leaves are pinnatifid, the 5 to 9 segments lin-

86

ear or lanceolate. The inflorescence is a terminal head with yellow-orange (sometimes reddish-purple) ray flowers and a columnar disk, gray at first and changing as it matures to purplish brown. The fruit is an angled winged achene.

The leaves and flowers of this plant can be used to brew a pleasant tea.

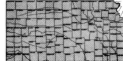

JUNE–AUGUST

◄ **Grayhead Prairieconeflower**

Ratibida pinnata (Vent.) Barnh.

(COMPOSITE FAMILY)

Grayhead prairieconeflower is an erect perennial 2–5 ft tall arising from a woody rhizome or short caudex with solitary to branched stems having minute, appressed hairs. The alternate leaves are pinnatifid, with lanceolate to lobed to entire segments, and loosely hirsute. The heads are borne on naked peduncles and have drooping yellow rays and a protruding ellipsoid disk. Prior to the opening of the disk florets, the disk is an ashy gray, turning brown following opening of the disk florets. The fruit is an angled winged achene.

87

Clasping Coneflower ►

Rudbeckia amplexicaulis Vahl

(COMPOSITE FAMILY)

Clasping coneflower is an erect, loosely branched, glabrous annual 1–2 ft tall. The alternate leaves are entire to sinnuate-dentate, ovate or oblong, and with a clasping, cordate base. The heads are long-peduncled, with 5 to 10 yellow (sometimes partly orange or purple) rays and a dark, cone-shaped disk. The fruit is a subterete achene without a pappus.

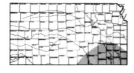

◄ Blackeyedsusan

Rudbeckia hirta L.

(COMPOSITE FAMILY)

Blackeyedsusan is an erect biennial or short-lived perennial 1–2½ ft tall with highly branched, bristly-pubescent stems. The alternate leaves are usually sessile, elliptic to oblong to oblong-ovate, firmly pubescent, entire-margined or shallow-toothed, and reduced above. The solitary heads are borne on long peduncles which terminate the branches and have long yellow or orange-yellow rays and an ovoid dark brown disk. The fruit is an equally quadrangular achene without a pappus.

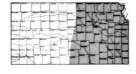

◄ **Browneyedsusan**

Rudbeckia triloba L.

(COMPOSITE FAMILY)

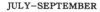

Browneyedsusan is an erect, short-lived perennial 2–4 ft tall with highly branched stems having appressed, stiff hairs. The alternate leaves are thin, sharply toothed to subentire, moderately appressed-hirsute, and ovate to subcordate. The lower leaves are often deeply 3-lobed. The solitary heads are borne on long peduncles which terminate the branches or arise from the upper leaf axils. The rays are yellow to yellow-orange and the disk dark brown. The fruit is an equally quadrangular achene with a minute crown as a pappus.

MAY–JUNE

◄ **Prairie Groundsel**

Senecio plattensis Nutt.

(COMPOSITE FAMILY)

Prairie groundsel is an erect perennial 6–18 in. tall arising from a branching rhizome or short caudex. The alternate leaves are wooly when young and glabrate at maturity. The basal leaves are closely spaced, toothed to pinnately lobed, and oblong to ovate. The upper leaves are sparse, linear-lanceolate, and commonly deeply pinnately lobed. The heads are terminal in a more or less flattopped inflorescence. The rays and disk florets are yellow to yellow-orange, the head ½–¾ in. in diameter. The fruit is a narrow flattopped achene with bristles on the angles.

This plant can cause poisoning of livestock, but is rarely eaten. Since it appears early in the growing season on pastures that have been grazed heavily, it may be the only green plant available and thus consumed.

89

◄ **Wholeleaf Rosinweed**

Silphium integrifolium Michx.

(COMPOSITE FAMILY)

Wholeleaf rosinweed is an erect perennial 3–6 ft tall arising from a woody caudex or rhizome. The opposite leaves are sessile, lanceolate to ovate, and toothed or entire on the margin. The terminal inflorescence is of clustered heads with yellow ray and disk florets. The involucral bracts are broad with slightly reflexed tips. The fruit is an obovate winged achene.

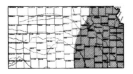

JULY–AUGUST

◄ **Compassplant**

Silphium laciniatum L.

(COMPOSITE FAMILY)

Compassplant is an erect perennial 3–8 ft tall with coarse, stiff hairs. The alternate leaves are deeply pinnatifid or bipinnatifid, clustered at the base, and with stiff hairs, particularly on the main veins. The upper leaves are reduced in size and may be entire. The inflorescence is racemelike of several heads with yellow ray and disk florets. The fruit is a broad achene, winged and notched.

The leaves of this plant commonly align, with the edges in a north-south direction. The plant also is resinous throughout, the exudate being chewed as gum. This plant is most commonly found in hay meadows or other ungrazed areas, since livestock will seek it out.

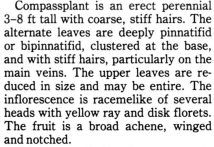

◀ **Cup Rosinweed**

Silphium perfoliatum L.

(COMPOSITE FAMILY)

Cup rosinweed is an erect perennial 4–8 ft tall with a stout, square, mostly glabrous stem. The opposite, toothed leaves are deltoid with clasping leaf bases, the upper pairs of leaves having their bases grown together to form a cup. The terminal flattopped inflorescence has heads with yellow ray and disk florets. The fruit is a variously notched winged achene.

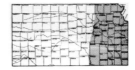

JUNE–OCTOBER

◀ **Buffalobur Nightshade**

Solanum rostratum Dun.

(NIGHTSHADE FAMILY)

Buffalobur nightshade is a highly branched, erect annual ½–1½ ft tall, yellowish-pubescent and yellow-spined throughout. The alternate leaves are 1–2 pinnatifid, the rounded segments irregular. The inflorescence is a lateral racemiform cyme of flowers with 5 united spiny sepals, 5 united yellow petals, and 5 yellow stamens, one larger than the rest. The fruit is a subglobose yellow berry enclosed by the persistent, sometimes adherent, spiny calyx.

This plant is commonly found in disturbed areas and in the first year of plant succession on "go-back" areas.   **91**

◄ Tall Goldenrod

Solidago canadensis L. var. *scabra* (Muhl.) T. & G.

(COMPOSITE FAMILY)

Tall goldenrod is an erect perennial 3–5 ft tall arising from long, creeping rhizomes. The grooved stem is more or less puberulent, particularly above the middle. The alternate leaves are sessile, sharply to finely serrate, lanceolate, and puberulent. The inflorescence is a pyramid-shaped panicle with recurved branches, the heads all pointing outward. The small heads have yellow ray and disk florets. The fruit is a bristle-tipped achene. Indians in Utah and Nevada ate the seeds of this plant.

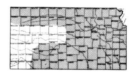

Missouri Goldenrod ►

Solidago missouriensis Nutt.

(COMPOSITE FAMILY)

Missouri goldenrod is an erect perennial 1–2 ft tall arising from creeping rhizomes, glabrous throughout. The alternate leaves are firm, prominently 3-veined, oblanceolate below, and reduced and lanceolate to linear above. The margin is serrate toward the tip of the blade. The inflorescence is a recurving 1-sided raceme with the heads pointing outward. The small heads have yellow ray and disk florets. The fruit is a linear-cylindric achene.

The leaves of this plant can be dried and used for tea or as a potherb. The ground leaves or the boiled leaf extract have been used as an antiseptic lotion. The leaves have also been used in salad in Arizona.

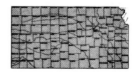

◄ **Ashy Goldenrod**

Solidago mollis Bartl.

(COMPOSITE FAMILY)

Ashy goldenrod is an erect perennial 1–2 ft tall arising from creeping rhizomes, canescent throughout. The alternate leaves are 3-nerved, elliptic to oval, sessile, entire, and the lower ones reduced and soon deciduous. The inflorescence is a terminal 1-sided raceme of small heads with yellow rays and disk florets. The fruit is a small short-haired achene.

◄ **Stiff Goldenrod**

Solidago rigida L.

(COMPOSITE FAMILY)

Stiff goldenrod is an erect perennial 1–3 ft tall arising from a short rhizome, densely to sparsely pubescent throughout. The alternate leaves are harsh and leathery, the lower ones petiolate with oval to oblong blades and sparsely toothed on the margin. The upper leaves are sessile, smaller, and ovate to oblong. The lower leaves form a large overwintering basal rosette early in the season prior to flowering. The terminal inflorescence is flattopped, dense, and composed of yellow heads of numerous disk florets and 10 or more well-developed rays. The fruit is a small glabrous achene.

93

SEPTEMBER–OCTOBER
Showywand Goldenrod ▶

Solidago speciosa Nutt.

(COMPOSITE FAMILY)

Showywand goldenrod is an erect, unbranched perennial 2–3 ft tall arising from a sturdy rhizome. The stem is coarsely hairy in the inflorescence, but glabrous to slightly hairy below. The alternate leaves are lanceolate, leathery, and toothed on the margin. The lower leaves are relatively large and the upper ones reduced. The terminal inflorescence is composed of spirally arranged heads forming a dense plume-like panicle unlike the 1-sided inflorescence of most goldenrods. The ray and disk florets are yellow. The fruit is a small glabrous achene.

Seldom does one find this plant in bloom that numerous bumblebees are not taking nectar.

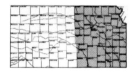

JUNE–AUGUST
◀ Slender Greenthread

Thelesperma megapotamicum (Spreng.) O. Ktze.

(COMPOSITE FAMILY)

Slender greenthread is an erect, slender perennial 1–3 ft tall arising from creeping rootstocks. The opposite leaves are usually twice-pinnately divided into linear segments. The upper leaves are entire and filiform. The inflorescence is a solitary rayless head of yellow disk florets. The fruit is a spindle-shaped achene.

The leaves of this plant make a tasty tea which also has been used in the Southwest as a wash for chafed skin, to reduce fever, and as a diuretic and vermifuge. A reddish-brown dye may be made from the leaves and a yellow dye from the flowers.

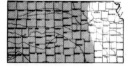

◄ **Western Salsify**

Tragopogon dubius Scop.

(COMPOSITE FAMILY)

Western salsify is an erect biennial 1–3 ft tall with milky juice. The alternate leaves are in a basal rosette the first year and on the erect stem the second. They are grasslike and clasping at the base. The inflorescence is a terminal head with only yellow ligulate florets. The fruit is a small achene with a large plumose pappus.

The mature head of this plant resembles a giant dandelion with the plumose pappi forming a large ball. These plants typically close the inflorescence during the day, giving the appearance of a goat's beard. The roots of this plant have the flavor of oysters or parsnips and may be eaten raw or cooked. The juice has also been used for chewing gum and for treating indigestion.

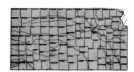

JUNE–SEPTEMBER

Flannel Mullein ►

Verbascum thapsus L.

(SNAPDRAGON FAMILY)

Flannel mullein is an erect biennial 2–6 ft tall, densely pubescent throughout. The first-year leaves are large, spatulate to elliptic-spatulate, and thick, forming a basal rosette. The alternate leaves of the flowering stem are oblong or oblanceolate and reduced in size compared to the lower ones. The inflorescence is a dense terminal spike of yellow flowers. The yellow corolla has 5 fused petals and 5 lobes. The reddish anthers are conspicuous. The fruit is an ovoid capsule with many seeds.

This plant is an herbalist's dream, with many ailments falling under its powers. Flannel mullein has been used to treat respiratory and alimentary ailments, external ulcers, toothaches, earaches, piles, gout, warts, and diarrhea. Other uses for the plant include boiling the flowers in lye to make a hair dye, feeding the seeds to fish to stupefy them so they may be caught by hand, and placing the leaves in shoes to provide warmth.

The Romans dipped the stalks in tallow and burned them as torches and the American Indians smoked them for bronchitis. The leaves were also used to make a tea which was fed to cattle for respiratory ailments. The seedheads are often seen in dried arrangements. This plant has been called "The Great Mullein"—little wonder!

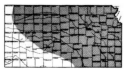

96

K E Y / *Orange Flowers*

1a. Margin entire
  2a. Tubular corolla, 195
  2b. Free petals, 141, 193
1b. Margin not entire
  2a. Toothed, 141
  2b. Pinnatifid, 178, 195
  2c. Lobed, 211

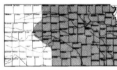

JUNE–JULY
Butterfly Milkweed
Asclepias tuberosa L. ssp. *interior* Woods.

(MILKWEED FAMILY)

Butterfly milkweed is a stout perennial 1–2 ft tall with 1 to several erect to ascending villous or hirsute stems. The linear to lanceolate to oblanceolate alternate leaves are 1½–3 in. long, numerous, strongly pubescent, and with entire margins. The flowers are arranged in 3 to 9 flowered, terminal, solitary umbels or arranged in a flat-topped inflorescence of several umbels. The 5-parted corolla, ¼–⅜ in. long, is yellow to orange-red. Hoods are colored similar to that of the corolla. The fruit is a follicle (pod) 2½–4 in. long and sparsely pubescent.

Though a milkweed, the plant does not have milky juice, but clear, latex-like juice. The root of butterfly milkweed is enlarged, giving it the species name *tuberosa*. The common name is derived from its ability to attract butterflies and many other insects. Those insects unwittingly play an important role in cross-pollination. Pollen sacs (pollinia) attached to a Y-shaped structure (translator) are located in slits between the anthers and become attached to the legs of visiting insects. Upon visiting another plant the pollinia are sloughed off and other pollinia picked up. However, many insects are unable to pull free of the slits and die on the flower.

Medicinal uses for butterfly milkweed are varied, but bronchial and pulmonary diseases seemed most often treated with this herb. Pleurisy treatment gave it the common name of "pleurisy root." It has also been used as an expectorant, emetic, and to promote perspiration. At least one author has described the young shoots as a tasty morsel.

◄ **Hairy Gromwell**

Lithospermum carolinense (Walt.) MacM.

(BORAGE FAMILY)

Hairy gromwell is an erect, bristly perennial 1–2 ft tall of 1 to several stems arising from a red-juiced, strong taproot. The alternate leaves are linear-lanceolate to oblong, broadening toward the base and covered with short, stiff hairs. The inflorescence is a dense raceme of orange-yellow flowers. The salverform corolla is of 5 united petals with 5 distinct lobes. The fruit is a hard, shiny, white nutlet.

K E Y / *Pink Flowers*

1a. Flowers with free petals (polypetalous)
  2a. Regular corolla (radial symmetry)
    3a. Simple leaves
      4a. Margin entire, 73, 209
      4b. Margin not entire, 22, 35, 57
    3b. Compound leaves, 112, 204
  2b. Irregular corolla (bilateral symmetry)
    3a. Plant viny, 206
    3b. Plants not viny, 63, 197, 203
1b. Flowers with fused petals (sympetalous)
  2a. Regular corolla (radial symmetry)
    3a. Alternate leaves
      4a. Simple leaves
        5a. Margin entire, 30, 198, 200, 201
        5b. Margin not entire, 20, 73
      4b. Compound leaves, 205
    3b. Opposite leaves, 52, 205
  2b. Irregular corolla (bilateral symmetry), 207

◄ **Illinois Tickclover**

Desmodium illinoense Gray

(PEA FAMILY)

Illinois tickclover is an erect perennial 2–4 ft tall arising from a deep taproot. The stem is finely pubescent with hooked hairs and alternate, pinnately trifoliolate leaves. The leaflets are ovate to rhombic-ovate, nearly glabrous above, and pubescent with hooked hairs below. The inflorescence is a sparsely branched raceme with small light pink to purplish pea flowers. The legume is a loment, breaking into 1-seeded sections with hooked hairs.

No plant in the prairie scatters its seeds more efficiently than the tickclovers. The hooked hairs on the pod cling to any animal or person passing by.

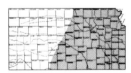

101

◀ Blacksamson Echinacea

Echinacea angustifolia DC. var. *angustifolia*

(COMPOSITE FAMILY)

Blacksamson echinacea is an erect perennial 1–3 ft tall arising from a thick black root. The stem is slender and rough-pubescent, with alternate, entire leaves, the lower ones petiolate and the upper sessile. The petiole and leaf blade are rough-pubescent and lanceolate to linear-lanceolate with almost parallel venation. The inflorescence is a solitary composite head with pink ray florets. The hemispheric disk has reddish-brown scales or bracts exceeding the disk florets. The sharp-pointed bracts produce a prickly knob. The fruit is an acutely angled, grayish, naked achene.

The root of this plant contains compounds that reduce pain. By chewing a bit of the root the tongue is numbed. Indians used this plant for toothaches, burns, wounds, and sore throat. The root extract is reported to be an antidote for rattlesnake bite, a remedy for blood poisoning and cancer, and a blood purifier. Pharmaceutical companies purchase quantities of the root for medicines.

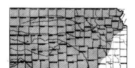

◀ Bush Morningglory

Ipomoea leptophylla Torr.

(MORNINGGLORY FAMILY)

Bush morningglory is a bushy perennial 2–4 ft tall arising from a huge turnip-shaped taproot weighing up to 25 pounds. The root may be 1½ ft in diameter and 3–4 ft long. The alternate leaves are linear and nearly sessile, slanting upward. The axillary flowers have a pink funnel-form corolla and resemble the common morningglory.

102

The fruit is an ovoid, long-pointed capsule.

The root of this plant can be eaten raw, roasted, or boiled or it can be dried for future use. The younger roots are the best for eating purposes.

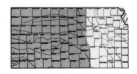

◄ **Rush Skeletonplant**

Lygodesmia juncea (Pursh) Hook.

(COMPOSITE FAMILY)

Rush skeletonplant is an erect, highly branched perennial 1–2 ft tall. The plant is glabrous throughout and has milky juice. The alternate leaves are linear and distantly spaced, the upper ones reduced to awl-shaped scales. The terminal inflorescence is of ligulate heads with 5 pink florets. The ligules have 5 teeth at the tip. The achene has a tawny pappus of soft hairs.

The stems of this plant often have bladderlike insect galls. The milky juice of the plant provides a chewing gum when coagulated. Mexican children have collected the small yellow balls that form on the plant and chewed them for gum, which turns bright blue on chewing. American Indians used extracts from this plant for eyewash. The plant has been reported poisonous by stockmen in Montana and Utah.

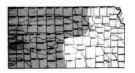

103

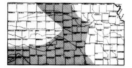

◀ **Silky Prairieclover**

Petalostemon villosum Nutt.

(PEA FAMILY)

Silky prairieclover is a tufted perennial 1–2 ft tall and grows in dense clumps. The stems are densely villous and very leafy. The alternate leaves are pinnately compound with 7 to 15 oblong leaflets. The leaflets are entire, densely villous, and glandular-punctate beneath. The inflorescence is composed of many cylindric spikes crowded with rose-purple to pink flowers. The corolla is not pealike, but has 1 large petal borne on a capillary claw and 4 others reduced to staminodes, also borne on capillary clawlike filaments. Each flower is subtended by a bract. The fruit is a thin-walled legume enclosed in a persistent calyx.

JUNE–AUGUST
Arkansas Rose

Rosa arkansana Porter

(ROSE FAMILY)

Arkansas rose is an erect, trailing, or climbing perennial shrub 1–4 ft tall, prickly throughout. The alternate leaves are pinnately compound with 9 to 11 obovate to obovate-oblong gla-

104

brous leaflets with dentate margins. The inflorescence is a flattopped cluster of light pink to red 5-petaled flowers with distinct yellow stamens. The fruit is an urn-shaped structure, commonly called a hip, which turns bright red at maturity.

Rose hips can be eaten raw, stewed, candied, or as preserves; they are also used to make a tea. The petals can be candied or eaten in salads. Arkansas rose has the same pleasing aroma as that of cultivated roses.

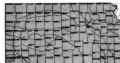

MAY–JULY

◄ Catclaw Sensitivebriar

Schrankia nuttallii (DC.) Standl.

(PEA FAMILY)

Catclaw sensitivebriar is a prostrate to semiprostrate perennial 1–2 ft tall with strongly ribbed stems covered with hooked prickles that bend downward. The opposite leaves are bipinnately compound with 4 to 8 pairs of pinnae and 8 to 15 pairs of leaflets, oblong to elliptic in shape. The inflorescence is a spherical axillary head of numerous flowers with 4 or 5 united pink petals. Seldom is the corolla seen, since the 8 to 10 pink stamens per flower far exceed the corolla, forming a fuzzy ball. The legume is linear, 2–4 in. long, ribbed, and with hooked prickles on the ribs.

The leaves of this plant are touch-sensitive, closing when handled or during high winds.

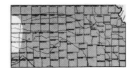

105

JULY–SEPTEMBER
◄ **Smoothseed Wildbean**

Strophostyles leiosperma (T. & G.) Piper

(PEA FAMILY)

Smoothseed wildbean is a twining or trailing annual, appressed-pubescent throughout. The alternate leaves are pinnately compound with 3 linear to narrowly ovate leaflets. The inflorescence is a single- to few-flowered head of pink-purple pea flowers. The fruit is an elongate, pubescent, subterete legume.

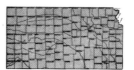

JUNE–SEPTEMBER
◄ **American Germander**

Teucrium canadense L. var. *virginicum* (L.) Eat.

(MINT FAMILY)

American germander is an erect perennial 2–4 ft tall arising from a slender rhizome with a pubescent stem. The opposite leaves are ovate-lanceolate to lanceolate, petiolate, pubescent, and dentate on the margin. The inflorescence is a terminal spike of pink to purplish-pink flowers. The corolla is tubular and bilabiate with a darker purplish-pink throat. The upper lip is 4-lobed and reduced, the lower, 5-lobed and prominent. The fruit is composed of 4 nutlets.

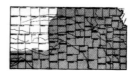

K E Y / *Red Flowers*

◄ Scarlet Gaura

Gaura coccinea Pursh.

(EVENINGPRIMROSE FAMILY)

Scarlet gaura is an erect perennial 1–3 ft tall with 1 to several stems that are canescent, puberulent, or glabrous. The alternate, entire leaves are lanceolate to narrowly oblong and finely pubescent. The inflorescence is a spike of 4-petaled flowers grading from white to red. The sepals are separate and sharply reflexed. The perianth is born on a stalk (hypanthium) prolonged above the ovary. The fruit is a hard, obovoid, indehiscent capsule.

The leaves of gaura are soft and pliable to the touch.

◄ Cardinalflower

Lobelia cardinalis L.

(BLUEBELL FAMILY)

Cardinalflower is an erect, usually glabrous perennial 1–3 ft tall. The alternate, simple leaves are lanceolate to oblong with a serrate or dentate margin and are usually sessile. The inflorescence is a raceme of red, bilabiate, tubular flowers. The upper lip is split into 2 lobes and the lower into 3. The fruit is a 2-celled, many-seeded capsule.

This plant has milky juice and is reputed to be of medicinal value, but poisonous. Nervous diseases, convulsions, asthma, tetanus, and other nervous disorders have been treated by *Lobelia* species. Pawnee Indians used the plant as a love charm.

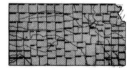

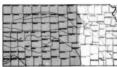

Scarlet Globemallow

Sphaeralcea coccinea (Pursh) Rydb.

(MALLOW FAMILY)

Scarlet globemallow is a branched, erect to semidecumbent perennial 6–18 in. tall with densely stellate-pubescent stems. The alternate leaves are deeply 3-parted, the divisions commonly lobed. The leaf is grayish-pubescent with stellate hairs. The flowers are clustered in short, leafy racemes. Flowers ranging in color from red to salmon have 5 free petals and a distinct stamen column. The fruit is a globose capsule of densely stellate carpels.

K E Y / *Green and Greenish-White Flowers*

1a. Leaves narrow, 214
1b. Leaves broad, 213, 215, 216

Spider Antelopehorn

Asclepias asperula (Dcne.) Woods. var. *decumbens* (Nutt.) Shinners

(MILKWEED FAMILY)

Spider antelopehorn is a decumbent perennial 6–12 in. tall with several stems arising from a single crown. The alternate to whorled leaves are lanceolate and leathery. The inflorescence is a solitary umbel with greenish flowers. The greenish corolla is upright, not reflexed as with other milkweeds, and the hood purple. The follicles are erect and resemble a small antelope horn.

111

JUNE–SEPTEMBER
◄ Narrowleaf Milkweed

Asclepias stenophylla Gray

(MILKWEED FAMILY)

Narrowleaf milkweed is an erect perennial 1–2 ft tall growing from a tuberous root with slender pubescent stems and milky juice. The upper leaves are alternate and the lower opposite, narrowly linear, and glabrous. The inflorescence is composed of several axillary umbels with greenish-white flowers. The corolla lobes are reflexed. The fruit is a slender follicle with tufted brown seeds.

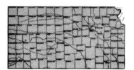

JUNE–SEPTEMBER
◄ Green Milkweed

Asclepias veridiflora Raf.

(MILKWEED FAMILY)

Green milkweed is an erect to ascending (sometimes decumbent) perennial 1–2 ft tall with thinly pubescent stems and milky juice. The opposite (rarely a few alternate) leaves are leathery; oval, obovate, or oblong; and wavy and scabrous on the margins. The inflorescence is of axillary sessile umbels with light green flowers and a reflexed corolla. The follicles are slenderly lanceolate with tufted brown seeds.

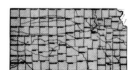

◄ **Green Antelopehorn**

Asclepias viridis Walt.

(MILKWEED FAMILY)

Green antelopehorn is an ascending, essentially glabrous perennial 1–2 ft tall with several stems arising from a single base. The alternate leaves are oblong or lance-oblong and leathery. The inflorescence is of clustered terminal umbels of greenish flowers with purplish hoods. The follicle resembles a small antelope horn and has brown tufted seeds.

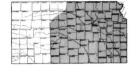

113

GLOSSARY

A—prefix meaning without.

Achene—a small indehiscent fruit, 1-celled, 1-seeded; ovary wall closely encloses the seed.

Actinomorphic—radially symmetrical.

Acaulescent—stemless or appearing stemless.

Acuminate—gradually tapering to a long point.

Acute—abruptly tapering to a short point.

Alternate—placed singly at a node; borne at intervals at different levels.

Angled—a projecting or sharp corner, particularly of stems and fruits.

Annual—living 1 year or less.

Anther—the pollen-bearing portion of the stamen.

Apetalous—without petals.

Apical—of the apex or tip.

Apomictic—reproducing without sexual union.

Appressed—lying close and flat against.

Arcuate—curved or arching.

Aril—an appendage growing at or about the hilum of the seed.

Articulate—jointed.

Asymmetrical—not symmetric.

Attenuate—long tapering to a slender point.

Awn—a terminal bristlelike appendage of a plant part.

Axil—the angle formed between 2 plant parts, especially leaves, stems, and pedicels.

Axillary—arising from or pertaining to the axil.

Barbed—having reflexed short bristles or other pointed appendages.

Barbellate—finely barbed.

Basal—located at the base of a plant or organ.

Berry—a pulpy, fleshy fruit developed from a single ovary and having immersed seeds.

Bidentate—having 2 teeth.

Biennial—living 2 years.

Bifid—2-cleft.

Bilabiate—2-lipped.

Bipinnate—doubly or twice pinnate.

Blade—the expanded terminal part of a leaf, petal, or sepal.

Bloom—the whitish, often waxy, coating of a plant part.

Bract—a modified or specialized leaf subtending a flower or part of an inflorescence.

Bristle—stiff, rigid, thick hairs.

Bulb—an underground leaf bud enclosed by specialized fleshy scales or coats.

Calyx—the outer whorl of flower parts; collective term for sepals.

Canescent—having fine, close, grayish pubescence.

Capillary—hairlike.

Capitate—headlike; forming a dense cluster.

Capsule—a dry, opening fruit of 2 or more carpels.

Carpel—a modified leaf forming a simple pistil or 1 member of a compound pistil.

Caudex—the short thickened basal portion of the stem of a perennial plant with an herbaceous top.

Caulescent—having a well-developed stem.

Cauline—of the stem.

Ciliate—with marginal hairs; fringed.

Clammy—damp, soft, and sticky.

Claw—the narrowed base of some sepals and petals.

Cleft—lobed about halfway to the middle.

Column—the united filaments of the mallow family.

Composite—a member of the composite family.

Compound—made up of 2 or more similar parts.

Compound leaf—composed of 2 or more separate leaflets.

Conduplicate—folded lengthwise.

Cordate—heart-shaped.

Corm—the enlarged solid base of a stem.

115

Corolla—the inner whorl of showy flower parts (perianth leaves); collective term for the petals.

Creeping—growing horizontally along or beneath the ground.

Crenate—with shallow, round teeth.

Crisped—irregularly curled along the margin of the leaf.

Crown—the root-stem junction or the leafy head of a tree.

Cuneate—wedge-shaped.

Cyme—a convex or flattopped inflorescence, the central flowers blooming first.

Deciduous—falling at the end of the growing season or following performance of a function.

Decompound—more than once compound or divided.

Decumbent—stems prostrate at base, upright elsewhere.

Deflexed—bent or turning sharply downward.

Dehiscence—opening of fruits, anthers, or other parts along sutures.

Deltoid—triangular-shaped.

Dentate—toothed.

Digitate—spreading outward from a single point like fingers on a hand.

Dioecious—having male and female flowers on separate plants of the same species.

Discoid—disklike; refers to heads with only regular, tubular flowers in the aster family.

Disk—the middle portion of the head, especially in the aster family, made up of tubular, regular florets.

Dissected—divided into slender segments.

Divergent—spreading.

Ellipsoid—football-shaped.

Elliptic—like a flattened circle.

Entire—without teeth, lobes, or divisions.

Erose—margin irregularly notched, as though gnawed.

Exserted—extending beyond.

Fascicle—a small cluster arising from a common point.

Fertilization—the union of the pollen nucleus and the egg.

Filament—the stalk of the stamen on which the anther is borne.

Filiform—threadlike.

Floccose—with loose, wooly tufts of hairs.

Floret—the individual flowers of the composite head.

Foliolate—pertaining to leaflets in a compound leaf.

Follicle—a dry fruit that opens along only 1 suture.

Fruit—the ripened ovary and attendant parts.

Fused—united by normal growth.

Gall—a mass of undifferentiated plant tissue produced as a result of insect action.

Genus—a group of related species.

Glabrate—nearly hairless.

Glabrous—without hairs; smooth.

Gland—a structure that secretes nectar or volatile oils.

Glaucous—covered with a bloom.

Globose—spherical.

Habit—growth form.

Habitat—the set of environmental and physical factors under which a given species grows.

Hastate—arrowhead-shaped.

Head—a dense flower cluster in which the flowers arise from a common point.

Herbaceous—pertaining to plants with the aerial portion not surviving the winter.

Hip—the fruit of the rose.

Hirsute—with spreading hairs.

Hispid—covered with stiff, bristly hairs.

Hoary—covered with fine, whitish, appressed hairs.

Hood—a segment of the corona of milkweed flowers.

Hypanthium—an expansion of the receptacle, often carrying the sepals, forming a tube; fleshy parts connecting the flower to the ovary.

Incised—sharply, deeply cut.

Indehiscent—fruits not splitting at maturity.

Inflexed—bent inward.

Inflorescence—a flower cluster or a floral axis with its appendages.

Internode—that portion of the stem between the nodes.

Involucre—one or more whorls of bracts subtending a flower or inflorescence.

Irregular flower—a flower in which members of the calyx or corolla are unlike; having bilateral symmetry.

Keel—a longitudinal ridge along the center of an organ.

Labiate—lipped.

Lacerate—torn.

Lanate—wooly.

Lanceolate—lancehead-shaped.

Lanceoloid—pertaining to a lance-shaped solid body such as a fruit.

Lateral—borne on the side.

Latex—milky juice of some plants.

Leaflet—one segment of a compound leaf.

Legume—the fruit of the pea family; dry pod, dehiscent along 2 sutures.

Ligulate—having a flattened, outward spreading appendage of the corolla of the outer florets of a composite head.

Ligule—a flattened, outward spreading appendage.

Linear—long and narrow, the sides essentially parallel.

Lip—the upper or lower division of a 2-cleft, irregular corolla.

Lobe—the usually rounded segment of an organ.

Loment—a legume that breaks into 1-seeded segments.

Membranous—thin, pliable, and usually translucent.

-merous—a suffix pertaining to composition of the floral parts, 4-merous meaning floral parts in fours.

Midrib—the central or main vein of a leaf or similar structure.

Monoecious—stamens and pistils in separate flowers on the same plant.

Nerve—vein of a leaf or similar organ.

Node—the area on a stem where leaves, branches, or flowers arise.

Nutlet—a small nut, commonly the fruit of the borage, mint, or verbena families.

Obcordate—oval-shaped and deeply lobed at the apex; opposite of cordate.

Oblanceolate—lancehead-shaped, with the broadest part toward the apex.

Obligate—limited to a specific relationship.

Oblong—longer than broad and having parallel sides.

Obovate—egg-shaped, with the broadest end toward the apex.

Obovoid—same as obovate, but pertaining to solids.

Opposite—in pairs at the same node directly across from each other.

Orbicular—circular.

Oval—broadly elliptical.

Ovary—the seed-bearing structure of the pistil.

Ovate—egg-shaped, the basal part broadest.

Ovoid—same as ovate, but pertaining to solids.

Ovule—that part of the ovary that contains the egg and upon fertilization becomes the seed.

Palmate—deeply lobed or divided and radiating from a single point.

Panicle—a compound or branched inflorescence with pedicellate flowers such as a branched raceme.

Pappus—the modified calyx-limb of the composite family represented as a crown of bristles, hairs, or bumps, persistent on top of the achene.

Parted—cut nearly to the base.

Pedicel—the stalk of a single flower in a cluster.

117

Peduncle—the stalk of a solitary flower or flower cluster.

Perennial—living more than 2 years.

Perianth—the collective term for the corolla and calyx together.

Petal—one of the floral leaves of the corolla, usually showy.

Petiole—the leaf stalk.

Petiolate—having petioles.

Petiolule—stalk of a leaflet in a compound leaf.

Phyllaries—bracts of the involucre below a composite head.

Pilose—covered with soft, spreading hairs.

Pinnae—primary divisions of a pinnately compound leaf.

Pinnate—having branches, lobes, or leaflets arranged along 2 sides of a central axis.

Pinnatifid—with lobes arranged pinnately.

Pistil—the female reproductive structure of a flower composed of the stigma, style, and ovary.

Pith—the spongy center of an exogenous stem.

Plicate—folded lengthwise, as a fan.

Plumose—featherlike.

Pod—dry, dehiscent fruit.

Pollination—the transfer of pollen from the anther to the stigma.

Pollinium (pl. Pollinia)—a mass of coherent pollen as found in the milkweed family.

Polypetalous—having separate petals.

Pome—a flesh fruit, like an apple, formed from an inferior ovary with several locules.

Prickle—small weak spines, outgrowths of the epidermis.

Prostrate—lying flat on the ground.

Puberulent—minutely pubescent with small hairs.

Pubescent—having hairs on the surface.

Punctate—having translucent dots.

Raceme—an inflorescence with pedicelled flowers upon a common axis.

Racemose—racemelike.

Rachis—the axis of an inflorescence or compound leaf.

Ray—the strap-shaped corolla of the composite family.

Receptacle—the swollen terminal end of a peduncle or pedicel; the disk- or dome-shaped structure of the composite family that bears the florets.

Recurved—curved downward or backward.

Reflexed—bent abruptly downward or backward.

Regular—pertaining to flowers bearing radial symmetry.

Reniform—kidney-shaped.

Resinous—producing resin.

Reticulate—netlike veins.

Retrorse—directed downward or backward.

Rhizome—an underground stem.

Rhombic—with the outline of an equilateral oblique-angled figure.

Rootstock—a rhizome or rhizome-like structure.

Rosette—a cluster of leaves radiating from the stem from about the same point in a circular form.

Rugose—wrinkled.

Sagittate—arrowhead-shaped.

Salverform—of tubular corollas that are trumpet-shaped (flared at the apex).

Scabrous—rough.

Scales—a reduced leaf or bract.

Scape—a naked flowering stalk arising from the ground.

Scapose—having a scape.

Seed—ripened ovule.

Senescence—death.

Sepal—the unit of the calyx.

Serrate—a sawtoothed margin.

Serrulate—finely sawtoothed.

Sessile—borne directly on the stem or other structure without a stalk.

Sheathing—surrounding the stem or other plant organ.

Simple—a leaf with an entire margin; an unbranched inflorescence; a one-celled pistil.

Sinuate—having a wavy margin.

Sinus—the indentation between 2 lobes.

Spathe—a large bract covering the inflorescence.

Spatulate—spoon-shaped.

Species—a group of like individual plants differing from each other only slightly.

Spike—an inflorescence in which the flowers are sessile on a central axis.

Spine—a sharp-pointed, woody projection.

Spur—a tubular or sawlike projection, usually from the calyx or corolla.

Squarrose—having the parts recurved at the end, usually of phyllaries.

Stamen—the pollen-bearing structure of a flower composed of the filament and anther.

Staminode—a sterile stamen; structure without an anther, corresponding to a stamen.

Stellate—star-shaped.

Stigma—the part of the pistil located at the end of the style that receives the pollen.

Stipe—the stalklike support of the pistil.

Stipule—a bractlike or leaflike appendage arranged opposite to or at the base of the leaf petiole or leaf.

Stolon—a trailing stem, rooting at the nodes.

Strigose—having appressed straight stiff hairs.

Style—the usually elongated portion of the pistil between the ovary and the stigma.

Subcordate—somewhat heart-shaped.

Suborbicular—somewhat circular.

Subtend—placed directly under a plant part.

Subterete—somewhat or almost cylindric.

Succulent—fleshy and thickened.

Sulcate—grooved.

Symmetrical flower—a flower in which any plane passed through its center divides it into mirror images.

Sympetalous—having united petals.

Taproot—primary descending root, usually thickened.

Tawny—tan-colored.

Terete—cylindric.

Terminal—at the tip.

Throat—the opening of a tubular corolla.

Tomentose—densely matted with hairs.

Trifoliolate—having 3 leaflets in a compound leaf.

Tuber—an enlarged underground stem, typically a food reserve organ.

Tuberous—having tubers.

Tufted—having many stems arising from a common rootstock or crown.

Umbel—an inflorescence with the pedicels arising from a common point. (In a compound umbel, the peduncles arise from a common point, each supporting an umbel.)

Undulate—wavy margin.

Utricle—a bladdery, 1-seeded fruit.

Valve—one of the parts into which a capsule splits.

Verticellate—whorled.

Villous—having long, soft hairs.

Whorl—3 or more leaves, flowers, or bracts arranged in a ring or circle at a node.

Winged—having a thin expansion bordering or surrounding an organ.

Wooly—having a dense cover of long, soft, matted hairs

Zygomorphic—capable of division into mirror images along one plane passed through the center.

REFERENCES

Anderson, Kling L., and Clenton E. Owensby. 1969. Common names of a selected list of plants. Kans. Agric. Exp. Stn. Tech. Bull. 117-R.

Barkley, T. M. 1968. A manual of the flowering plants of Kansas. Kans. State Univ. Endowment Assoc., Manhattan.

———. 1977. Atlas of the Flora of the Great Plains. Ames: Iowa State Univ. Press.

Coats, Alice M. 1968. Flowers and Their Histories. London: Adam and Charles Black.

Curtin, L. S. M. 1947. Healing Herbs of the Upper Rio Grande. Santa Fe: Univ. of New Mexico.

Fernald, M. L. 1950. Gray's Manual of Botany, 8th ed. New York: American Book.

Fox, Helen M. 1933. Gardening with Herbs. New York: Macmillan.

———. 1953. The Years in My Herb Garden. New York: Macmillan.

Gates, Frank C. 1932. Wild flowers in Kansas. Kans. State Board Agric. Rep. 204-D.

Gleason, Henry A. 1952. The New Britton and Brown Illustrated Flora of the Northeastern United States and Adjacent Canada. Lancaster, Pa.: Lancaster Press.

Harrington, H. D. 1954. Manual of the Plants of Colorado. Denver: Sage Books.

Harris, Ben Charles. 1961. Eat the Weeds. New York: Crown.

Irvin, Howard S. 1961. Roadside Flowers of Texas. Austin: Univ. of Texas Press.

Johnson, James R., and James T. Nichols. 1970. Plants of South Dakota grasslands. S.D. Agric. Exp. Stn. Bull. 566.

Kirk, Donald R. 1975. Wild Edible Plants of the Western United States, 2nd ed. Healdsburg, Calif.: Naturegraph.

Kreig, Margaret. 1964. Green Medicine. Chicago: Rand McNally.

Krochmal, Arnold, Russell S. Walters, and Richard M. Doughty. 1969. A Guide to Medicinal Plants of Appalachia. Upper Darby, Pa.: USDA.

Lander, G. D. 1912. Veterinary Toxicology. Chicago: Alex. Eger.

Lommasson, Robert C. 1973. Nebraska Wild Flowers. Lincoln: Univ. of Nebraska Press.

McGregor, Ronald L., Ralph E. Brooks, and Larry A. Hanser. 1976. Checklist of Kansas vascular plants. State Biol. Surv. Kans. Tech. Publ. 2.

Muenscher, Walter C. 1948. Poisonous Plants of the United States. New York: Macmillan.

North, Pamela. 1967. Poisonous Plants and Fungi. London: Blandford.

Peterson, Roger T., and Margaret A. McKenny. 1968. A Field Guide to Wildflowers. Boston: Houghton Mifflin.

Stevens, William Chase. 1948. Kansas Wild Flowers. Lawrence: Univ. of Kansas Press.

Stuhr, Ernst T. 1933. Manual of Pacific Coast Drug Plants. Lancaster, Pa.: Science Press.

UNESCO. 1960. Medicinal Plants of the Arid Zone. Paris: UNESCO.

von Reis Altschud, Siri. 1973. Drugs and Foods from Little Known Plants. Cambridge: Harvard Univ. Press.

SCIENTIFIC NAME INDEX

121

COMMON NAME INDEX

123